MY LANCASHIRE CHILDHOOD

by
Catherine Rothwell

OWL
BOOKS

First published July 1993 by
Owl Books
P.O. Box 60
Wigan WN1 2QB

ISBN 1 873888 40 6

Designed and Typeset by Coveropen Ltd., Wigan.

Text produced via high resolution DTP Palton 11.5 on 13.5 pt

Printed and bound in Great Britain.

CONTENTS

This book has been put together with love for the children of today: Eleanor; James; Joanna; Jocelyn; Patrick; Philip and Tor. To them I say,
"I have spread my dreams under your feet. Tread softly be-cause you tread on my dreams".
Of the children of yesterday only two remain. Living but a handspan from poverty, we children never knew of it, nor were we aware of the wealth we shared. Charles in particular, who gave me leave to weave his memories, enriched our lives with his painting and music. All would agree that dedication goes to mother, profound, troubled, yet serene, a rock at the heart of the matter. She seemed to make everything possible.

Scattering Ashes at Pilgrim's Cross

The curlew cries down the wind, his
  soul-haunting, echoing loneness.
Here to the bone are my beginnings,
Etched in the weather-worn stone.

Our brothers followed the standard bearer,
Went marching with Legions o'er moorland
where cotton grass bends,
And the Roman road's territory vanishes
Into world's end.

Out of Holcombe, blowing wet, blowing dry,
Like the sheep disguised as boulders,
Day long we laughed and called to one another
Under the shaggy, changing Lancashire sky.

The curlew cries down the wind.
Fly, darlings, fly!
Their ashes soar, flurry my face,
But, setting the pace,
Together, road-eager they vanish.
They mingle in space.

Catherine Rothwell

INTRODUCTION

In the 1920s and early 30s when most of the following impressions were formed it was difficult to get work. A typical joke of the period was when one of the great number of unemployed hearing cries of distress as he walked along the canal bank, hurried to see a man struggling in the water.

"Where do you work?" queried the man on the towpath and on being told, raced off to that address leaving the man to drown.

"One of your men has been drowned in the cut," he said. "I've come for his job."

"Too late — the man who pushed him in has got it."

"Doctors' wives die and cobblers' children go barefoot" were other cynicisms at the time. In recent years these have been levelled at me for not sorting out my own family tree but helping others to do theirs. The closest relations which my brother and I best recalled fleetingly are in the rudimentary family tree that follows, if such it can be termed. But we were nonetheless interested in the shadowy, unrecorded past and the characters who peopled it, people whom we had never met. Indeed, in some ways these seemed the more intriguing. In childhood, the sensations, sights, sounds, smells are inseparable to be soaked up like a sponge; many experiences apparently lying dormant until perhaps years later they are triggered-off to suddenly surface with a feeling of *deja vue*. Rather than the stereotyped family tree, a collection of impressions seemed preferable, the deepest being expressed in photographs all of which are linked with a Lancashire childhood.

The Edward Hoghton of Belthorn and Yate & Pickup Bank, Darwen, was Innkeeper of the Dog Inn. (It is interesting to note from indentures that Hoghton became Houghton on the advice of some lawyer at some indeterminate date.)

The first Edward had several properties besides the inn, i.e. a row of cottages, two farms, a butcher's shop and a small, early, cotton textile mill in which in that inventory of his possessions the machinery is stated to be "very old". It is recorded that an occupant of one of his cottages filled the interstices between the millstone grit flagstones on the parlour floor with lead, so that he might enjoy long, uninterrupted rocking in his chair.

The Hoghton family in the 1890's. This photograph, the oldest we have, is of great interest, showing Uncle William Edward holding the kettle, great-great-grandmother Hoghton, Annie who was William Edward's wife, and my father Clement standing beside the swing. The gathering is on the occasion of a picnic in the garden at Belthorn or Downham. The family photographs in this book were taken by Clement using his large, heavy-plate camera which he made himself, on wooden tripod, draped with a black cloth.

Edward worshipped in the Established Church at Haslingden Grain but later in the 1880s they attended Emmanuel Church, Oswaldtwistle, where members of the family are buried under a worn, thin headstone of white Carrara marble, while Clement occupies a new grave alone. On the South wall of Emmanuel is a jewel-glowing, stained glass window dedicated to Edward. The Hoghtons and the local Belthorn clergyman had a bitter disagreement over something ("I hold with the Headmaster, right or wrong.") Such outrageous talk to a Hoghton would damn the cleric for ever, yet they were loyal to the Establishment. Grandmother Catherine raised her brolly to the statue of Disraeli in Ormskirk Market Place shouting above costermongers' cries: "Good old Dizzy." William Ewart Gladstone was set down by great grandfather "Ned" as "Bloody Billy" over the General Gordon affair at Khartoum, yet as a child I distinctly remember a marble bust of the great statesman at the old family house. Like the de Hoghtons who helped to build places of worship and enjoyed a true catholicity in their circle of friends, the Belthorn Hoghtons stoutly believed in tolerance for all.

The eldest son of the eldest son was always christened Edward, another of that name being known as the Dancer since he excelled in the pastime. He left a son Edward and a daughter Elizabeth Agnes, neither physically strong. The son probably suffered from hypothermia since his habit was to sit in front of a roaring fire. Folks nearby could smell his clothes scorching in the heat. One day this Edward's hat and dashing clothes arrived in a big tin trunk together with all sorts of other paraphernalia. The hat of superfine black felt could be folded up. Edward must have resembled Giuseppi Verdi when wearing it. My brothers loved dressing up as pirates in this garb and there was an exquisite beaded silk bodice for me. We all thrilled at these mysterious items with their romantic whiffs from the past but mother was hurt, knowing that they had descended on defenceless poor relations as items to be got rid of.

Catherine Cronshaw refused to marry Edward until he got rid of the Dog Inn, deciding that an innkeeper could not make a desirable husband. To his two sons caught swimming in the mill dam the erstwhile innkeeper was reported to have said, "Wait until your mother hears of this" — indicative of who wore the trousers in that Victorian household, and it is a sad fact that with the parting of the old inn began the salting away of the rest of the Hoghton property.

Jonathan Cronshaw, Catherine's first husband, could not have been a poor man. Two articles of furniture I recall would have pleased Arthur Negus: a mahogany long case clock and a walnut inlaid William and Mary bureau of superfine cabinet work. Unfortunately all Clement Houghton's possessions at the year of his death, 1954, fell into the hands of his elder brother whom Clement, in a moment of great weakness, had named his executor. These and the many works of art collected by Clement's brother Jonathan, who died of typhoid fever after eating mussels, were lost to our family forever and the house sold for a song.

Catherine had a half sister Polly who revelled in late nights, entertainment, trips to Blackpool, Bolton and Wigan by cha-

Jonathan Cronshaw Houghton, Blackburn Market Inspector, (far left) was an uncle I never knew for he died in the prime of life from typhoid fever after eating mussels. His hobby was collecting antiques and paintings. I recall that he managed to acquire a David Cox water colour at a reasonable price, a Venetian vase and a set of Spode china amongst other lovely items.

rabanc, not to mention hot pie, cow heel and chip suppers. In the thirties Polly graduated to weekend trips to the Continent, indulging in the same fare. Her rather low tastes must have been a trial to Catherine who, I suspect, was a snob. Certainly Polly was jolly whereas Catherine was perpetually disapproving.

A solid-gold watch and a beautifully carved, long-handled parasol of silk were amongst Catherine's personal possessions.

> *"How sweet my childhood days were,*
> *How merry and free . . ."*

This from one of Catherine's poems which has survived. Her "dear, kind uncle" was a member of the well-placed Garnett family.

Mother, who rarely sat down, had a hard, wooden chair with a plywood seat. "Lady Hornby", an upholstered Chesterfield, was reserved for father but, already having seen better days, she expired on a groan of springs and kapok the night the marble fireplace fell upon her. Luckily we were all abed but the soot from the chimney wrecked the room.

Mother was born here in 1888 and told us many stories about her early days. We loved climbing Seat Naze and going "Up Water". On the way we thrilled at an ancient haunted house. We got to Waterfoot by travelling from Bury on "Puffing Billy", passing through rural stations like Edenfield, Stubbins, Summerseat, their gravel platforms beautifully kept by regular sweeping. Station names were picked out in flowers or white chippings.

Emma Worswick was our maternal grandmother and here she is in her best hat, photographed by my father in his Waterfoot Studio. As a girl she had lovely Titian red hair and wore small pieces of good jewellery. She considered Lancashire comedians "vulgar". By the way she pronounced it you knew what she meant and she had no time at all for the grammar schools. I fell from grace the moment I won a scholarship.

Belonging to choirs was important in our family. We heard about the Deign Layrocks (larks) of Rossendale who went up into the hills singing. Mother had her happiest years with the Chapel Choir and its outings. Charles was a chorister before he became organist. The Clitheroe Glee Singers, here seen with their splendid solid-gold guards, were known to our parents.

Widowed for the second time, Catherine and her son Clement, who both disliked the country, escaped to Blackburn to a double-fronted house in Brantfell Road. Queen's Park was a favourite retreat.

Clement married Ethel Fielden, our mother, whose father was a master baker from Rossendale. Mother's grandmother, Grandma Worswick, had a general store on Burnley Road which then carried the monopoly for Cadbury's chocolate in the whole valley. I remember her daughter Emma with shiny, auburn hair well into old age. Grandad Worswick, described as the "please yourself sort", sailed twice to U.S.A. when it was an adventure. On returning home the second time for more money from the shop till, he insisted on the whole family embracing the Shaker sect which was founded by a lady in Manchester, an early feminist who believed the Holy Ghost was of her sex. It was flourishing in the 1850s in the States, the men of the movement wearing aprons or 'brats' whilst the women wore plain dresses and white bonnets like the early Quakers. Grandfather Fielden fell from grace. Seeing the band of the Salvation Army approaching, he roared to the world at large, "There goes Salvation" and, smiting his breast, "Here goes damnation." Grandad Worswick, obviously a born ecumenical leader, played the violin in the gallery of the Methodist Church and at choir sermons was happy to play in the Anglican building of Newchurch. That was the time of the famous Dean Layrocks, whose singing fame spread far and wide beyond Pendle Hill.

Father's 'side' for some obscure reason seemed to consider themselves superior clay, but what we children could never forgive was that they were not nice to mother. Her side of the family, more human and likeable, was visited by boarding "Puffing Billy" at Bury railway station and chugging along the rural line through Summerseat, Stubbins and Edenfield. Charlie had his favourite sweetmeat, a raisin bar, whilst I sucked away at my delight, a small bar of Fry's Cream Chocolate. We were with mother and thus we were happy and she was happy too. For a short while she was going home.

Catherine Rothwell
Poulton, 1993

ACKNOWLEDGEMENTS

I am indebted to Lancashire Library and Manchester Polytechnic for allowing me to use two photographs. Also to Stanley Butterworth; Bob Gibson; John R. Houghton; Katherine Hall Houghton; Sheila Houghton; Eric Mills; Ron Severs; Ralph Smedley; Brian Williams; Diana Winterbotham.

CHAPTER 1

The Railway Children

THE wall was a rock garden; it was part of our play-ground and it was also a grand stand for viewing the passing trains. Daily, except Sunday, throughout the year we were on the wall at half-past seven in the evening, standing or sitting, waiting for the loaded coal train to pass up the incline. In early childhood I sat there, supported by mother's arm, my elder brother (by six years) standing beside me. Later, aided by the height of the dustbin, I declined mother's help, and a little later still I climbed the wall using the crannies as toe holds. "Driver, driver", shouted my brother, whilst I, giving support to the fireman, called loudly for his favoured attention. Every evening we stood there waving. Only absence from home, illness or inclement weather prevented our attendance. But, as the years passed we no longer shouted, merely waved and, finally came the evening when even that was too much. Thereafter we no longer watched, we had grown older and wiser in the ways of the world.

As little children this routine was anticipated: after it we were washed and went to bed, but five minutes before the train was due we were waiting, heads turned to the left from which direction we should see the first billow of smoke rising from the long tunnel. Steadily climbing and rounding the curve, the thunderous blast of the exhaust was joy to our ears and the pungency of mingled steam and burning coal sheer pleasure to our noses. From the tall smoke stack the shower of red-hot grit was flung high into the air, amidst the belching black smoke and momentarily white vapour. This awesome sight was enhanced by the mad racing of the driving wheels as they failed to grip the rails from time to time, and at this the red sparks would fountain higher above the billowing wake. Thod-thod, thod-thod went the following trucks, and often the screech from a locking brake-shoe, and the judder, judder, judder as the brake handle beat wildly up and down under the inexorable pull of the locomotive. On Winter nights with rain we still watched through the kitchen window. Our heroes, standing under the shelter of tarpaulin sheet slung from the edge of the cab canopy, chuffed by on their iron monster, and the red glare from the open firebox door was a friendly island of light in the fretting waters of surrounding darkness.

By the four acres of land over that wall we watched the

We loved the "softly panting train" so much we could have been called the Railway Children. On Summer Wakes Week holiday, staying at Blackpool in lodgings overlooking Central Station, Edward could not be coaxed from the "digs". He spent all his time watching trains arriving and departing.

14

As the first girl, I had to be called after my paternal grandmother who in return bequeathed to me her long, gold chain and solid gold watch. The outfit I am wearing was knitted by Aunt Annie Ward—all in green wool. I liked it, even the snuffing- out hat, because green was and is my favourite colour.

march of the seasons. On the opposite side of the cutting was a wild service tree, and when a green mist surrounded the bare branches we knew that Spring had arrived, just as we were certain of Whitsuntide when the sickly pink rhododendrons flowered. A patch of helianthus also sprang up in Summer, and I for one, found its odour strange and disturbing. Surpassing all these were the privets that had been left untended, and growing unchecked to a height of nine or ten feet, became a mass of creamy white fragrance in early July. I have several times heard it said that privet blossom is offensive smelling, but its heady, never-forgotten tang is beloved of the humble bee. After all these years whenever I catch a stray whiff of privet, or see the flowers turning brown on their stalks lying in a shallow pool of rain on an August pavement the days of childhood are evoked, and I am grateful.

To the left the wall ran, by a series of rising courses, beneath a row of black poplar trees whose leaves were plagued by caterpillars in Summer. Beyond these trees stood a large wooden shed, at one time a firelighter factory, and at another a garage, with a solitary pump proclaiming Pratt's petrol. The building was patched with cast-off enamelled steel plates bearing past and present advertisements: Stuart Horizontal Engines, Stephen's Ink, Cherry Blossom Boot Polish, Benson's Watches. One's nose was titillated by the smells that clung to the building: lubricating fluid with its overtones of castor oil, naphthalene always, and creosote in the slow, quiet hours of a hot Saturday afternoon. In Winter mist seemed to drift round the place, harsh, hostile and sour with soot.

And yet there was the wall, and over it, the railway cutting, and the fall of the year; there was the stone edge of the platform glistening wet with wind-driven rain, with the long paths of amber light reflected from the distant signals; there was the hot, sweet smell of lamp oil, and the shuttered guide lamp that fluttered blue in the rising wind before turning to a yellow steadiness, and there was the never-ceasing moan of the telegraph wires, the insistent rattle of a wantonly-swinging gate, and the faraway whistle of an engine.

The street was quite short beginning at the railway bridge, where it changed its name, and ascended an incline with stone setts all the way, to help the poor dray horses we were told. Buff gritstone pavements bordered it with worn flags and smooth kerbs not much higher than the carriageway itself. At the lower end where our terraced cottage stood, but four doors away, was a gas lamp and the maker's mark was the sign of a crab; the lamplighter's son went to my school. This four-sided lantern crowned with a copper cap was fitted with glass trapdoors. Through these the lamplighter thrust his long staff surmounted with a brass cylinder and bearing a pilot light. As he pushed over the wing tap there was a loud pop and the twin mantles flamed into a greenish-yellow glare. Only at nightfall in the darker months could I, like R.L. Stevenson, wait for my Leary* from the parlour window, for in Summer the lan-

*Robert Louis Stevenson, poet and author mentions the lamplighter of his childhood as "Leary".

terns were collected, and conveyed to the Town's Yard on what appeared at casual sight to be a ladder of wood mounted on a hand cart, each lantern placed upright between each two rungs.

A few yards further on, in the middle of the road, was the barred grating of a manhole, and we children were bidden never to stand over or near it "Because of the bad air". We did though, at times, since the sound of falling water below our feet fascinated us. From where did the water come and to whence did it flow? Only later did we learn about sewers.

On the opposite side of the street I remember three things amongst others: the sandy foundations of the railway bridge and the cutting with hundreds of blue lupins in Summer; a tall laburnum tree, and a run of old-fashioned roses, like a white Dorothy Perkins. Next came a Congregational Chapel in half an acre, surrounded by a palisade of upturned railway sleepers and partly by an incomplete brick wall. Gossip said that this place of worship had been built against the wishes of the Lord of the Manor. During one of his absences, for he had properties elsewhere, his agent had sold the land to the chapel sponsors and the building was a *fait accompli* when the noble gentleman returned. He never forgave the trustees. One can quite believe this story for it is well known that he cost the railway company a pretty penny when they wished to cross his land in the early years of the railway age, for he insisted that the line should only be allowed if it passed beneath his private park, and tunnelling through sand can prove very awkward.

Before we children became regular attenders at the Established church we went to the Sunday school opposite, and occasionally attended Morning Service in the chapel on the floor above. There was a wide spiral staircase with stained glass windows of floral patterns, and at the top a heavy curtain, sign of bourgeois comfort against draught, shrouded the door. The minister wore striped trousers and a frock coat, white shirt with stiffened front and cuffs and a grey silk necktie. He had also a silk hat, spats over kid leather buttoned boots and pince-nez spectacles. He was the essence of dignity, and to me as a small child he impressed far more than the pink-faced, tubby Anglican priest I was later to meet, who never seemed to take off his cassock unless to don an alb, amice, chasuble and all the rest of High Church gear.

At the top of the street, one on either side stood corner shops: on the right a tripe shop and on the left a fried fish shop.

The tripe shop had originally been a private dwelling, last one of a terrace facing the main road, and the window of the front room still carried its original six panes. Some shops never got beyond this stage but were kept limited in size. A house doing baking only, rather than a baker's shop, was quite popular then, often run by a widow left in impecunious straits, a cottage industry doing nothing beyond baking bread and teacakes, and a cushion against hard times. For several years I helped to collect the bread and delicious bread it was, baked in the coal oven of a cottage kitchen range.

A solitary woman served in the tripe shop: never was I served by another person. No food was ever displayed in the window. Instead two or three pot plants filled the space, resting on a floor of plain tiles. Behind the plants a discreet gingham check curtain, gathered on a tensed cord and supported by small wooden posts at the extremities, hung down, the whole about eighteen inches high. One entered, and the bell, clanged by the striker attached to the opening top edge of the door, brought out the shopwoman, dour and middle-aged.

"Yes?"

"A pound of best seam tripe, please," placing the money on the narrow, high counter, just above a child's eye-level. Whilst the meat was cut, so white and almost odourless one looked at the pictures on the opposite wall, those one had seen so many times before, a pair of strongly coloured prints depicting various breeds of parrots.

"Here you are."

"Thank you."

Another clang and one was out again descending to the pavement by three semicircular-steps.

The fried fish shop opposite had a bigger trade, noisier, more talkative (since one had to wait) and more bustling. The owner and his wife ceaselessly plied their daily trade without ever seeming to rest or take holiday. Both had that well-tubbed, well- scrubbed look, and both were clad in spotless white overalls. The anthem sung in the choir seemed to refer to them,

What are these that are arrayed in white robes
And whence came they?

Here I must interpolate that in the times and places of which I write this creed of soapsuds, in a practical rather than literal sense, this much-scrubbing of bare woodwork seemed always to be taking place somewhere in the week. Pails of hot water, blocks of wire-cut Windsor pale primrose and blue mottled soap and reddened wet arms to the elbow, were sure to be seen in some food shop. The faint smell of citronella oil could often be detected before the week was out whether at the butcher's, with sawdust underfoot, or at the baker's (they scrubbed early), the fishmonger's (he scrubbed late), or the greengrocer (he was erratic and worked on a movable feast).

The proprietor and his wife moved to and fro before the chip range like officiating priests at the sacrificial altar dedicated to the god of the belly. At intervals the man would tend his twin coal fires from opposite ends, and into the

19

pans of boiling fat resting above those fires, would thrust a wire skimmer shallowly catching the fragments of charring chip bits. Again, he would grasp a chip, drawn to the surface in a wire cage, and test it between right finger and thumb for readiness. Less frequently a pail of whole peeled potatoes was forced through a steel chip machine by hand into a white enamelled colander below. Fish prices were low. Everyone ate fish on Tuesday and/or Friday in that area, Catholic or no, and consequently one could purchase a fish piece covered in golden batter for small cost. These also the man prepared carefully and then floated into the heaving, swirling fat. So, timed almost to the nearest second this frying routine continued throughout the day, apart from a brief rest in the afternoon, never hurried, never at a loss for something to do.

His wife sold and wrapped the food and helped the children who asked for 'Plenty of salt and vinegar, please' from a giant aluminium salt shaker and a porcelain-corked vinegar bottle. It was possible to sit and eat one's purchases at the cast iron, marble topped tables, indeed, for another 1d. one could make the meal a feast with a helping of boiled, parched peas, perching before it on a wooden stool, but when we called we were generally on our way home, and sit we never did.

Secured to the outside wall of the shop was a 1914-1918 street roll of honour, illuminated in vellum and fixed into a hardwood frame surrounded by a latin cross, and bearing the names of men who joined the services but who never returned to their homes in that street. For King and Country read the title, In Proud Memory. Other streets, too, had their memorials in a similar design, but before I was ten years old the majority of these cenotaphs had disappeared.

Behind the tripe shop stood a courtyard surrounded by two-up-and-two-down artisans' cottages, the space cobbled completely and entered by a gateway set in the front elevation of two adjoining houses. This was Gartside's Court. Another court, designated to the lower status of alley, and whitewashed all round to a height of eight feet, stood nearby. This area was generally avoided by my friends and me because of the rough boys who lived there. Upper rooms were reached from outside stone steps. Perhaps they had originally been weavers' homes, for their age showed in the stone floors — I was invited there once and had a cup of tea, from a most elegant cup and saucer — in the roofing tiles of Pennine sandstone and simple V wooden gutters. The courtyard of the alley was cobbled in a similar way to the Court, and I seem to remember a pump standing in one corner.

The only other building I knew well was Fred Jackson's grocery store and off-licence, more the latter than the former, though he did a fair trade in commodities and it was for these I made my visits. It stood half-way up the slight hill. It seems a little strange now that so many different proprietary brands of soap products were for sale, and not just the brand names of two or three limited manufacturers. There was Brook's Monkey Brand, a scouring block for scullery use; there was Ivy soap — "It floats" — and Dr. Lovelace's soap. Acdo block was cut in wafers for Monday's washing and Gossage's Beefeater Carbolic was kept by the kitchen sink for casual washing. All these in addition to those we still have, excepting the Hedley (later Procter and Gamble products) which did not meet the eye in our parts until just previous to 1936. Jackson's had a complete glass cupboard (formerly stocking a well-known brand of chocolate from the Big Three, Cadbury's, Fry's and Rowntree's) and it held many proprietary medicines to which the poorer off resorted for relief in sickness. However much the present National Health arrangements are full of shortcomings they are infinitely better than the woefully inadequate

21

'provisions' of the 1920s. Then one went "on the box" only in dire necessity; hospital was feared and side-stepped as far as one possibly could do so, and when regrettably and unavoidably it could not be averted the sufferer had to haggle with a petty official on the price he could afford to pay in that institution before he was allowed over the threshold. Consequently, the lowest-paid workers clung to faith in the power of manufacturing pharmaceutical chemists. How great the contrast between the poor and their local Member of Parliament, when they occasionally read in their local free press that he was being treated in a London Nursing Home for a minor ailment.

This one is Mr. Kidd's of Cheetham Hill. Mother walked miles from Heaton Park to Cheetham Hill, the nearest place having a "clinic" and baby centre. We bought oiled silk lint and Germolene from Mr. Kidd as one or another of us always had sore knees from falling. Father used to advise "leather knee caps" as worn by the many working horses of the day.

Throughout the year there were itinerant vendors of small-value goods: hawkers and door-to-door salesmen, keen after patronage, however trifling. One man comes immediately to mind since he came regularly every fortnight, year after year, but for three seasons of the year only, Summer being excepted. He wore a cotton union shirt without collar in lieu of which he wore a white, fringed silk muffler, which also helped to dispense with a necktie. A dark woollen overcoat over a blue serge suit covered him and on his head he had a check cloth cap. His hands were large, white and strong and had a most capable look about them. He carried a large rectangular wicker basket, a baker's basket, well-filled with crumpets and freshly-made, limp oatcakes, the whole decently covered with a white linen cloth. When it rained the basket wore a hat of black oilskin mackintosh gathered round the edges with elastic.

Every Monday passed by the "Sambone" man. That was the two-note call he seemed to enunciate walking alongside his small, light cart drawn by a donkey, with the woollen rags he preferred piled at the front high up and the rear of the cart low down, weighed there by the burden of white, cream and brown stones used to smarten outside steps. These he traded for rags or desirable rubbish or junk.

On Mondays, too, came the Clothes-prop man with unmusical call and four or five wooden clothes props for the washing line for sale.

The Ice Cream man from whose cart, pushed by hand, we were allowed to buy our two penny and one penny cornets lived in the street. Of a multitude of hokey-pokey men his barrow alone had an English name, and unlike the rest it was soberly painted and carried none of the fanciful scenes from an improbable mythology with festoons and cupids simpering at each corner. He was a tubby little fellow, and certainly worked for his money, pushing the heavy barrow mile after mile. The apron he wore was spot-

The rag and bone ["Sambone"] man with a donkey cart shouted, "Any old rags, bottles or jars, any rabbit skins, old chairs to mend?" The "rag and bone" man paid with donkey stones, cream and brown, which the women used to colour cleaned hearth stones, steps and the pavement immediately in front of their house door.

lessly white and so starched that the hem stood out from his body, not following his plump contours. It was quite as large as a baker's apron and had a capacious cash pocket, which, surely, could never have been full. I never saw him once without his cap whilst he was selling though I did know he had a bald head.

Once every Summer came the Herb seller bearing a large brown basket of sage and thyme. Once or twice I can remember he brought fragrant lavender in small bunches for the linen chest.

There was a Haberdasher person—it could be a man or a woman—carrying round a large fibre suitcase full of cards of pearl and cloth faced buttons; sewing cotton and button cotton; cards of darning wool and knicker elastic, hair nets, boot and shoe laces and needles and pins in paper; narrow machine-made laces and trimmings besides many other different items to such a degree that one would wonder how on earth **could** they fit into such a container!

The milkman who came each morning daily changed his tactics in Summer when he also came in the early evening, when one could enjoy a good cup of tea if perchance the morning's milk had turned sour in the thunderous weather—no refrigerators for working class in those days! He looked the horsey type and wore riding breeches, brown leather gaiters and a hacking jacket of woollen check. The graceful milk float, drawn by a chestnut horse generally carried two milk churns on one side and a large cylindrical, nickel-plated milk tank of a far-greater capacity, at least twenty gallons, I should say, on the other. This tank was fitted with a close-fitting lid beneath which, inside, two metal measures with crooked handles hung, not touching the liquid for the tank was never more than half full. A line

Morning and evening milk deliveries arrived punctually in every street, the milk still warm from the cow. Hung alongside the milk float were gill and pint measures, the milk being measured from a shining churn chained to the cart. Poured into a quart kit, this was carried into the house. The cart was beautifully, spotlessly varnished and the churns etc. scalded regularly.

25

of milk kits of differing sizes hung by their brass clips from the rail inside the float, stamped with the imperial measure and the owner's name. After he had measured the desired quantity one collected the milk at the door in an appropriate jug. By arrangement, though not as a general sale, he sold eggs and cream.

The seasons were known by their games, played in the Little Back behind the terrace, or, in Summer, in the street itself, or one which was at right angles to it. In tender childhood these games were all gentle: bowling hoops, whip and top, hopscotch, hide and seek, and skipping — this with a length of vegetable rope we had begged at the greengrocer's from off the boxes of Spanish oranges, thirteen for a bob, that entered the country about December. These games were generally played in the cooler seasons. Others: Ghost in the Garden, Buckets and Strides, Sly Fox, Old Woman of Botany Bay, and, surely, Marbles were less active and therefore more suitable for warmer weather. Later, when the girls withdrew to play only with members of their own sex the boys ganged together in Kick Can and Rally-O Relieve O, games that never seemed to finish, that were better played at night and which involved much running and calling from street to street. In Winter, too, each boy made himself a Winter Warmer which consisted of an empty four-ounce cocoa tin in which a nail was used to punch several holes in the lid. Inside, a piece of smouldering cotton waste was inserted and by judicious blowing one could produce a fair amount of heat and a great deal of smelly smoke. On the earth surface of Little Back the girls at play would scrape house interiors with a pointed stick drawing, in a stylised manner the things they would expect to find in their house. Alas, they all drew pots of gay pelargoniums on every windowsill (I can't remember any in that street), and proudly on the first floor appeared an elegant bathroom (which no house possessed) with an inner lavatory pan (when all the street had to retire outside).

26

We made Liquorice Water alias Spanish Juice. A four ounce or slightly larger medical flat bottle was fitted with a cork and filled with water into which small pieces of hard liquorice were added, and the bottle rested in a warm place between vigorous shakings. After a day the mixture was thick, brown and frothy and in this state was imbibed, if not with joy, then with satisfaction. Sweets seemed harder to come by in those days than they are to the average child now. As a special concession since Charles was in the choir, my parents allowed him Singing Toffee, limited to a halfpenny a week, and there seemed to be a great variety of choice with such slender means at one's disposal. Imagine asking for a ha'porth of fat ducks, green peas and new potatoes, and getting some of each in a triangular shaped bag!

CHAPTER 2

Tar Boilers, Shops and Whitsuntide

A S little tots, brothers and I, when so inclined, con-structed tents. There were two kinds we made: the Summer type for out of doors utilized a rectangle of hessian sacking, whose longer side was placed horizontally on a brick wall, and nailed there along the top edge at a conveni-ent height. Two broomstales, various lengths of string, and several tent pegs judiciously placed formed a canopy under which we conducted our palavers. The Winter tent con-sisted of two discarded full-length curtains, which were draped over a square dining table in the manner of a large tablecloth, the ends reaching the floor. Helping in the Winter camping game (we took our own refreshments in Summer), mother conveniently laid two freshly buttered currant tea cakes on a plate before the flap entrance for us to eat inside. To increase realism, for we were romantically inclined, we made a nodding acquaintance with the inclem-ent weather outside, especially when it was very squally, and would temporarily quit our tent and hide between the heavy draught curtain and the outside kitchen door. For some reason this had to be done on hands and knees, standing was not permitted, and with the door slightly ajar, we would peer round, inhaling deeply of the cold air, shivering in happy anticipation at the hardships without and the warmth and friendliness within.

Later tents were not essential: we would invent, pretend and dramatise whenever the need arose as all children do, if the materials were not to hand: it was often enough, if the grass was plentiful and dry in Summer to lie there and dream . . .

Ich ruhe still im hohen grunen Gras
I rest quietly in the tall green grass
Und sende lange meinen Blick nach oben,
And steadily look upwards,
Von Grillen rings umschwirrt ohn Unterlass,
Crickets ceaselessly stridulate around me,
Von Himmelsblaue wundersam umwoben.
And I am surrounded by a sky of blue.

Die schonen weissen Wolken ziehn dahin
The lovely drifting white clouds
Durchs tiefe Blau, wie schone stille Traume; . . .
Sail through the deep blue like beautiful quiet dreams; . . .

So wrote Hermann Allmers in his "Feldeinsamkeit", Solitude in Summer Fields. To lie lazily and watch the slow purposeful, silent procession of cumulus clouds, was sufficient pleasure in itself.

Like most children I became excited when I 'discovered' things that took my fancy, stimulated my imagination or stirred my sense of beauty. In themselves these things could be quite simple and might not have moved many children as they did me: a few mossy steps, seemingly coming from nowhere and projecting from an overgrown bank; an ancient gnarled tree of interesting shape; an uncommon fungus, especially if it had a highly coloured cap. A spring of water, cold and clear, rising from the earth and flowing through the forest of sphagnum bog moss to join the nearest stream down the hill would give me great delight.

It was mother who started us off and her vital and infectious curiosity in life made all learning pleasure, reading, writing and arithmetic included. Mother gave freely of her time; even during housework or shopping there was opportunity to draw our attention to something. She told us of the Yeomen of the Guard pictured on the packet of Gossage's Lifeguard Soap on washday, and explained why the good ship "Unity", a vessel of the Manchester Co-operative Society merchant fleet, should be sailing across a 3lb. packet of Federation Self-raising Flour every Wednesday baking day. She called us to listen to the sounds around us: the song of the lark in Farmer Hardy's fields; the call of the

Kersal Bar, Higher Broughton. From here by tram car we could get to Heaton Park which was a wonderful playground to range. Its extensive acres had belonged to the Earl of Wilton until Manchester Corporation purchased it for a public park. Its wild places we named romantically. There was the "rushy whip wood" where we collected rushes to plait. "Small Copper hollow" and the "Red Addy (Admirals) Walk" referred to butterflies. Temple Hill had an observatory. It was where I spotted my first Brimstone butterfly at the age of eight. The tram in the photograph is going to Eccles where the famous Lancashire Eccles cakes were made.

lapwing and the wind thrumming through the telephone wires as we walked up Hodges Lane; the hissing of the wind passing through yellowing, dried grasses on the steep bank of the reservoir. She pointed out ladies' smocks in the ditch and the heart shape of the lime leaves overhead with the sweet smelling of its flowers in July. One day, as we sat on a felled beech trunk eating a picnic tea after school she pointed to the vast bulk of the dirigible R34 air ship, passing high above us like a great silver sausage with the R.A.F., red, white and blue roundel on her hull.

There was interest in watching people perform their daily tasks in the community: bricklayers, road maintenance men, painters and the like. "Mr. Pinner" our name for the gentleman from the water board who visited the village streets every quarter and flushed the mains, was almost as commonplace as the policeman or lamplighter, and we took little notice as he passed by. On the way to school we might see someone not too common like a surveyor or a gang felling a dangerous tree, but when I attended a secondary school five miles away, by train, the chances of seeing something fresh greatly increased. For instance, at the station we travelled to was a large timber yard and I counted myself lucky when the man with the adze was working. With this heavy cutting tool wielded by the right arm in a chopping motion he "tooled down" the greater irregularities in tree trunks used for callender bowls (rollers used in textile and paper manufacture), and later to finer limits to be machined on a lathe. In his initial attack great chips of wood flew heavily around him but later, when the bowl seemed sufficiently cylindrical and finished he would still draw off long shavings. What a keen eye for symmetry he had and a sure, practised hand! I put this artisan in a similar class to that of the famous mediaeval painter who drew a perfect circle with one flourish of the wrist as a practical example of his skill.

Whooping cough, which many children caught in Winter at the most inconvenient times could be alleviated, old wives said, by walking twice round the gasworks. Equally efficacious was to linger in the vicinity of road works where a tar boiler was in use. The ailment is still with us but the remedies have disappeared, probably for good. Gas is now produced cleanly from the North Sea and there is no longer the falling rain of black grit, nor the intermittent belching of nigrescent smoke and hazy red flame from the horizontal retorts. One can no longer watch the busy saddle tank engines pulling loaded coal trucks nor indulge to the full in the stench of coal gas that clung everlastingly to the areas around gasworks. Whether the smoke, soot fall-out or smell of coal-tar acids now produced in the National Coal Board patent fuels plants (under the Clean Air Act — clean, that is, for all but the unfortunate persons living thereabouts) are as effective, for pulmonary complaints, we shall perhaps never know.

The tar boiler, always seen sooner or later at every street excavation or road maintenance, was a lumbering wheeled tank of large dimensions. It was provided with a tall chimney stack at one end and a firebox at the other, and was reminiscent of nothing so much as a small and simplified Puffing Billy stripped of its cranks and driving levers. A foot beneath the chimney projection was a huge tap from which the hot, melted tar flowed into the pails, scoops and other utensils used to carry the glistening jet black liquid. Where stone setts were the basic road material the tar, used as an amalgam, was poured into the interstices between the stones already half-filled with roadstone chippings. In later days tar coated the concrete surface of the road and used as an adhesive, held the stone chippings, in graded layers, scattered thereon.

Gas works and road works were most useful as diversions and helped to take the mind off wearying school mat-

Making the East Lancashire road, Swinton area, in the late 1920's. We loved the scent of hot tar, spread on roads and then gravel covered, to be followed by the heavy steam road roller. The smell of tar was supposed to help clear up colds and speed convalescence, as was walking by the sea as the tide came in.

ters. There were also other things that helped one to dilly-dally on the way.

There were three types of steam road engine that one might possibly, nay, one HOPED to meet on the road. First, the showman's engine with a curved canopy supported on four polished brass, barley twist pillars and, placed before the chimney, having a dynamo running by belt and pulley from the flywheel. The brothers and I remember watching for some considerable time, until we had to return home at sunset, whilst a gang struggled to save one of these engines from sinking for ever beneath the corner of a notorious swampy field. We assumed they saved it but later, two unfortunate house buyers were to bless their misfortune when later still they purchased the same patch of land, this time with a pair of semi-detached houses on it. The houses, like those built on sand that Jesus spoke of, fell.

The steam road roller resembled the showman's engine but in a more utilitarian way, and had large spoked wheels at the rear as had the showman's engine, but whereas the roller had a large roller on which one end of the boiler rested the other engine had a pair of wheels at the front. The third member of the trio was the haulage engine. It was smaller than its relations, had a vertical, smaller boiler, could raise steam more quickly, carry a greater load and move faster, too. It was used by heavy hauliers carrying flour, timber and the like, on its own wagon. Very occasionally one saw it pulling an extra long and heavy load on a trailer crocodile burdened with a giant boiler or condenser. Of these machines (apart from those carefully demonstrated in exhibitions since) nothing but the memory remains of whirling eccentrics, spinning governors and a smell of hot lubricating oil piercing the thin haze of smoke and exhaust steam and a following of eager, small boys, anxious to be offered, but never quite getting a free ride.

The horse as power for haulage (excepting those that

Young imagination boggled as to what these monsters could do if they ran amok so we made up stories about them. Juddering away, sinking into the mud with belts whirling, they were used to drive the merry-go-round when the annual Fair came to town and pitched on the Hayes. The same fields in Spring were golden with tall buttercups. They were also employed with harvesting, like Britannia, here working in Treales near Lytham.

brewers use partly as an advertising ploy) is an obsolete idea. Years ago they were commonplace but always impressive, especially in the combination of tandem, a well-matched pair of shires drawing behind them a large dray of grey cloth or finished paper in enormous rolls four feet or so in diameter, or a high load of esparto grass with its strong smell not at all like sweet country hay. Those horses were so familiar with their routes that they stopped and started without any promptings, and would show impatience at an overlong wait by sharply striking the setts with a right fore shoe.

Desire for change took us from the street to visit other areas of children's activities. I never knew why we went to one place (and only during Winter) unless it was to warm our hands against the end house of a terrace where there was a warm area where the kitchen fireback stood. Here we assembled, side by side, with our palms and backs flattened against the brickwork. We never played games there, nor shouted, for quietness was strictly observed; obviously we had discovered that provided we behaved in that fashion we were allowed on sufferance.

There were times when we walked to Willie Frazer's. He was the first man in the village, apart from the two doctors, to own a car. It was a 'Napier', a six seater open tourer with wire- spoked wheels and folding canvas hood and having long running boards fitted with aluminium treads. Perhaps there was a space on them for a shrouded spare wheel standing against the car side in a little curved channel something like an egg in an eggcup, if you know what I mean. Willie had the largest newsvendor's shop, and he always wore a tweed knickerbocker suit, with thick, woollen, double topped stockings and brown leather brogues which had a punched pattern on the toecap. He had a fair-sized moustache, curled just like the horns of a water buffalo, and waxed at the tips.

His shop had much treasure. We lined ourselves outside the windows, "bagging" this or that or the other, but inside excitement mounted as more wonders came into view. Here the most expensive toys and reading books, annuals and fascinating novelties were sold; here the largest boxes of Christmas crackers, here the most ostentatious Christmas decorations and here the most expensive wallets and boxes of stationery—not that we were interested in writing—that was work! Here, too, if one joined the Christmas Club one · went with one's parent to choose a book or a toy in the arranged price range. My brothers and I bought our set of Wonder Book annuals here, but one year I decided on a change and chose one quite unlike the usual run of children's books. It had the most fascinating covers in an all-over pattern, blue and white, of rampant gryphons, which I read had been copied from the original pattern in a London Museum — the V. and A., no less! I recorded the fact though it meant nothing to me then. "Was I sure," Willie asked me," was I **really** sure that I wanted that book called Number Two Joy Street?" Of course I was sure: the covers alone were exciting and a glimpse of the beautiful wood-engravings within (a form of art I had already learned to appreciate) stirred my imagination quite deeply; goodness only knew what lay within besides!

The authors' names were names and nothing more but I had set my heart on the book and would be unsatisfied until it was in possession, but notice who the authors were and all under one cover. There was Prince Rabbit (A.A. Milne); The Dragon at Hide and Seek (G.K. Chesterton); Lucy (Walter de la Mare); A Thing to be Explained (Lawrence Houseman); The Stranger (Hugh Walpole); A Cautionary Tale by Hilair Belloc and so many, many more. Edith Sitwell wrote a poem for it, and Rose Fyleman — The Princess of Kensington and They, respectively, if my memory is not at fault after this lapse of sixty years. It opened a new world to me. It was in it that I first heard of Sussex where so much beauty dwelt. No wonder I grew up to be a librarian!

Of course, that didn't stop me from reading penny comics, though by the time I had the book, comics were no longer staple fare, and Willie sold a whole selection of these: Jester and Funny Wonder on Saturday; Comic Cuts on Tuesday; Chips on Wednesday. Two others which we were not encouraged to read lest they brought disturbed sleep (they had a **slightly** stronger content) were Golden Penny and Butterfly. All the characters therein contained: Constable Cuddlecook, Weary Willie and Tired Tim, Sammy and Jackie the Circus Twins, Roland Butter and Hammon Egg, Mustafa Bunn and the Jam Sponge and all the rest amused us until twopenny magazines took over with Magnet, Popular, Wizard, Rover, Union Jack, Sexton Blake and Scout, Chums and Modern Boy. They certainly kept us reading, reading — and criticising.

Willie Frazer's was at the end of the village main shopping thoroughfare, Butterthorn Lane where shop design was about equally divided between the purpose built ones on the south side — not a good side for a shop but they could not choose since the other side had got there long before — and these, the north-facing shops. These latter had begun as private dwellings in the early 19th century and had then developed a trade in some commodity or other. It had then been justifiable to extend premises by the addition of a one-storeyed room from the front door, and this was clearly seen in some shops, for as the customer entered, the assistant, summoned by the clanging bell, descended the steps at the rear of the shop from the living quarters via the front entrance of the original house.

The largest shop was at right-angles to the lane, a grocery store, the Co-operative Society, in Stores Street. Like all grocers of the time the Co-op did much of their pre-packaging on the premises in clearly-distinguishable bags: sugar in blue sugar paper; washing soda in brown ditto; currants, raisins, and sultanas respectively in purple, magenta and yellow kraft paper. Cheese (unless in maker's pack) was sold only in absorbent cheese paper, on which the cheese, if in any way moist, had left bright yellow stains. Biscuits were seldom wrapped and could be viewed before purchase through the window above the square biscuit tin. Education was part of the Co-op self-improvement plan — as it still is, though by no means to the same extent — and our branch, like many another, had a department devoted to this social need. There was an upper room over the shop used as a library on Saturday afternoons, presided over by an elderly librarian, spectacled, and so interested in his books that I fancy he would have preferred to have been left alone to his love. The borrower presented himself at a window where a complete library list was handed out for him to make a choice. He could not browse and examine; there simply wasn't the room for space was at a premium. This is one reason why this library was in decline; another was that about this time many newsagents were setting up small libraries of light fiction: Sapper, Edgar Wallace, Sidney Horler, Ethel M. Dell, Jeffery Farnol and the like where one could borrow at a trifling cost a new book at each visit. The third reason was that a small county branch library was built in the village, but by that time I had left secondary school behind me. As I said there were other educational facilities: concerts and recitals; competitions and musical festivals; rambling and camping clubs and opportunities for economical holidays. All these were valued and put to excellent use. The sponsoring of passive entertainments by many present day firms is not quite the same thing. With the Co-op you HAD to take part if you wished to benefit— as I said before it was self-help in the best tradition.

Butterthorn Lane was a focal point, which was a place to

meet people one had not seen for some time. Annually it was the starting point and terminus of the Whitsun walks, those religious processions held at Pentecost and probably very similar to that one mentioned by Charlotte Bronte in Shirley. We did not, like her differing denominations, violently disagree; instead we all, Anglicans and Free Churchmen (our Roman brethren politely withdrew from the scheme) took our turn to lead the united procession of witness on an annual rota of precedence. What a day! What a festival so eagerly waited for, especially by the young ladies — with their new frocks, and those a little older with their new outfits! What bravely blaring brass bands! What a flaunting of florally-festooned texts! What boldly-borne banners breasting the breeze, each carried by two men whilst four young women strain at their two-colour banner

We always shopped at the Co-op and "Divi" was to us a fairy godmother. Mother's careful housewifery included hoarding Co-op dividend for rainy days. It bought me a white dress and patent leather shoes that fastened with pearl buttons in readiness for Whit Walks. Divi allowed two easy chairs to come in at the front door whilst "Lady Hornby" was trundled out at the back to a rag cart. It even paid the fees for one of us to attend grammar school. A wonderful institution!

cords like guy ropes to a tent, and keeping the billowing material upright bend their heads and place the palms of their free hands on the crowns of their large, picture hats, in a gallant effort to keep them on! The young damsels, from those newly entered into the kindergarten to those who have reached the middle school, loosely hold white ribbons and carry elegant baskets of fragrant flowers, charming all hearts as they are photographed by older friends again and again. Small boys, with unaccustomed brushed hair, held down by water or a little oil, more smartly dressed than salesmen from one of the more distinguished showrooms and sporting buttonholes of rose or carnation, proudly present themselves to relations and neighbours, collecting pennies in a breast pocket. Fathers in new suits; choir in surplices and servers in cottas of dazzling white, newly-starched by the ladies of the church; scouts, cubs, brownies, guides, rovers and rangers — all in neat uniforms; clergy in stocks and stoles and dog collars with prayers of thanks said silently for the warm, sunny weather, all gathered in Butterthorn Lane to testify by their presence that Christian unity, if not here and now was definitely on its way. Almost to the end of the second decade of the century each separate denomination returned to its own schoolroom after the procession to take afternoon tea, although, if the weather was really warm and no rain had fallen for some time, the Congregationalists took over a field for the afternoon and had a picnic tea. By the beginning of the thirties the preparation for this chore, which largely devolved on the ladies, especially the matrons, seemed to have become more than a little irksome. Serving tea to many children can be a hazard for new clothes so it was therefore abandoned by general assent. In any case tea parties were no longer considered a treat; even the long- established Tea Garden, which had been popular with the lower middle and artisan classes for the whole of the previous century was now in rapid decline.

40

We measured the year by the greater festivals of the Church and these were brought before us by the by-products of special fairings, perhaps not the ideal way, but it had a soundness in practice. Modern youth still partakes of some of these: Christmas with presents; Shrove Tuesday with pancakes and Easter with pace and chocolate eggs. We also observed Mid Lent or Refreshment or Mothering Sunday with little bunches of flowers for Mother and Simnel cake for the rest of the household. Then there was Palm Sunday (palm crosses) and Good Friday (hot cross buns). Some areas had extra celebration like Fig Pie Sunday (Blackburn) and Blackcurrant Sunday (Heywood) and the presentation of God cakes, triangular pastries filled with a spiced mincemeat filling in the town of Bolton. Every church and chapel had its 'Sermons' or Anniversary Sunday. We also remembered Ascension Day when the older children of the village school after attending church and

This Lancashire 1930s Carnival Day photograph gives you the lot: friendly "Bobby"; Morris dancers with the real McCoy "swishy" batons; brass band complete with "oompah" and Britannia, important beneath the Union Jack, ensconsed on a decorated coal cart.

41

morning day school, went on a picnic in a char-a-banc to a local beauty spot and picnic area.

A short distance from Butterthorn Lane was Big Croft. We generally avoided it for children there greatly outnumbered our gang from Little Back and in the croft we were regarded as trespassers and petty rivals. Here was other interest, though, in the being of Bert Fisher and his char-a-banc. To the ignorant the char-a-banc was nothing more than a perambulating clutch of church pews if you can imagine that, and the precursor of the motor coach, every pew or bank, a long, upholstered bench seat stretching the width of the vehicle. There was no central aisle running the length of the chassis; instead one entered by a half door on the near side. Every bench seat had its own half door — and there must have been up to six on each side in a larger char-a-banc, though there were smaller vehicles with only half that number and less than half the carrying capacity. With folded canvas hood, there were no side screens, we bowled along the quiet lanes with a respon-

The first charabanc I remember was drawn up outside the school yard ready to take the older children on a trip to Ashworth Valley. How I envied them! The roof was rolled back and they sat on bench seats. Charabancs must have gone out of fashion soon after as I only dimly recall the thrill of riding in one.

sible child seated against each door with its upright trigger or polished brass handle, as happy as happy could be, singing a song we had learned in school or a song of the moment heard in a seaside music hall. The pace was leisurely and limited to twelve miles per hour, certainly not suitable for a motorway!

CHAPTER 3

Foudroyant and Other Trips

ON a perfect summer's day in June 1897 Father and Grandfather set off from their hill-top village, Belthorn, above Blackburn, to make what was then quite a journey. Travelling by the Preston and Wyre steam railway, for the last five miles they had cantered over Fylde mossland in a high wagonette, arriving at the seaside resort of Blackpool as the sun went down. The news that Lord Nelson's historic flagship, the Foudroyant was anchored off there had travelled fast and like thousands more they wanted to see her.

In her day one of the most famous ships in the world, it was strange indeed that the country's number one playground by the sea should be the scene of her memorable wrecking.

For a fortnight the vessel, anchored three miles off North and Central Piers, was an object of interest to thousands of holidaymakers. Steamers and sailing craft had daily conveyed people to tread the decks and explore the Admiral's Cabin. "Flaming, thunderous, firestriking" was the meaning of the name of this most renowned of the wooden-walled ships of the old British Navy and she had lived up to it, making history under the greatest naval hero of all time, Horatio Nelson. Launched in the Spring of 1798 at Plymouth and christened after a captured French ship, Foudroyant was a sixty-gun two-decker. Lord St. Vincent wrote to Nelson: "She is the most perfect ship that ever swam on salt water." Standing on her decks, the unparallelled Admiral had made his greatest chase of the Genereux, urging the Captain to "crowd on every stitch of canvas and make the Foudroyant fly to the capture."

Twice in her career the ship was a refuge for the Royal families of Naples and Portugal. Fleeing from Napoleon, a sister of Marie Antoinette had hidden on board. The recovery of Malta also figured in the vessel's distinguished career.

Although in 1851 Foudroyant was extensively repaired, the sad day dawned when the ruthless Admiralty decision, "sold out of service to a Plymouth ship breaker" was announced. To save her from the even greater ignominy of being towed to Germany for firewood, rich man Mr. G.W. Cobb stepped in. He spent £20,000 on refitting Foudroyant, planning to exhibit her at many seaside resorts. Following a spell at Southport it was arranged that she would be Blackpool's greatest attraction in Queen Victoria's Diamond Jubilee Year, 1897. Fate provided a town which gloried in the spectacular with one of the most sensational occurrences in its eventful history.

In Nelson's day Foudroyant had a crew of 713 but as a show ship she was in the charge of 6 men and 20 lads, the latter dressed as jolly Jack Tars. Fooled by blue skies, Captain William John Robins paid no heed to warnings that if the wind rose, the Foudroyant could be in difficulty.

After a good Lancashire high tea, Clement and Edward, the latter one of a number who feared Captain Robins was courting disaster, walked to the beach. Clement, a mere boy, was to talk of the Foudroyant's wrecking for the rest of his days. He told me: "We saw her the night before the storm looking picturesque with her masts and rigging all trim and neat, her painted portholes looking like black and

45

white tile work. The setting of a calm sea was reminiscent of the old, romantic days of sea battles, when the great wooden ships came to grips with the French."

Unexpected and unannounced, the gale began that evening and by early morning, sailings on the 'Queen of the North' and for the Isle of Man were cancelled. Local historian Allen Clarke heard the wind howling amidst chimney pots. "There came a man with the news that Foudroyant had broken loose from its moorings and was drifting ashore. As I dashed out of doors I could see she was already aground, level with the Hotel Metropole. Foudroyant lay on her beam ends, huge waves sweeping her decks, watched by a seething mass of human faces concentrating on the death struggle."

The spectacular wrecking of Lord Nelson's flagship, The Foudroyant, off Blackpool in 1897 was witnessed by my father. Foudroyant timbers were made into souvenirs, jewel boxes, tables, walking sticks. Masonic Lodge furniture was made from the oak and copper. Medallions showing the ship were struck from metal. As the Foudroyant carried sixty cannons in three tiers, the damage caused by the violence of the waves was enormous.

Cracking like whips, first one, then another of her three masts snapped and toppled overboard, carrying yards and spars with them until only three stumps remained. For six hours the fate of the crew was uncertain but suddenly men were seen crawling towards the shelter of the poop deck. Borne slowly on the tide, it had been feared that the massive vessel would sweep away the Pier Jetty but this was mercifully averted by the current moving northwards.

Wheatley Cobb, writing to his mother from the Wellington Hotel, described how it had looked from the ship. "Floods of water swept through the shattered door of the Admiral's cabin. I had never seen waves like them . . . no one could have lived two minutes in that sea. Every internal fitting and bulkhead was swept away, the decks rent to pieces, timbers ripped in every direction and she bumped with such violence that the lower deck guns ploughed grooves three feet deep through the solid oak sides of the ship . . . A shout went up that the new lifeboat had put out. We got into the Samuel Fletcher and were landed in a crowd of several thousands."

Meanwhile Blackpool's enterprising Advertising Manager C. Nadin was busy telegraphing the news all over the country, bringing in trainloads of sightseers in search of souvenirs.

My Father found copper nails. Much of the wonderful timber was carted off and made into furniture, walking sticks, jewel boxes, whilst metal was melted down to become commemorative medallions, many of which survive.

Mr. Cobb employed a salvage company from Glasgow, striking an agreement that if the Company failed to refloat Foudroyant they could have the ship for £10 and be paid nothing. The guns and beautifully carved figurehead were recovered, the latter being preserved at Caldicott Castle, but the attempt to refloat was a failure.

Strangely enough, the unique Foudroyant had still not had the last word. Two further vessels were wrecked trying to salvage more timber and in the following November another raging sea smashed what remained of Foudroyant to bits, dismembering every oak, plank and beam.

According to Grandfather, and maybe even Nelson himself would have agreed along with other old salts in that huge crowd, it was fitting that such a great ship should bow out at the height of storm and tempest.

Few knew more of west coast sea lore than Grandfather. "The old warrior fought to the last," he said, unsurprised that after sailing the seven seas for a century, Nelson's "Dear Foudroyant" had finally been conquered by the furious capability of the Irish Sea.

Talking of trips, although there wasn't much "brass" to spare for our generation, mother seemed to work wonders in the way of food and outings, investing both with her rich store of imagination. I loved her lemon curd and the way she thinly sliced big jaffa oranges, layering them with sugar in a deep, cut-glass dish. Father was a great storyteller, especially when the rice pudding course came on. "Eat up and I'll tell you a Jimmy Eccles story," he would say, Jimmy Eccles having been his bosom pal. The stories were always about Belthorn, the village where he was born. One tale was so very long, little sister Sheila fell fast asleep with her golden curls in the pudding and the bowl.

I only ever remember accompanying father on one picnic. Typically he chose the depths of Winter when, on the spur of the moment, he had decided to take his two little girls in search of "a utick's nest." Needless to say, we never found it, but I still remember the mystery and the magic he wove into that trip to Heaton Park. We settled by a tree stump and "laid the table", spreading out our drinks, cake, fruit and sandwiches. Well wrapped up like two scarlet balls, my sister and I have no recollection of feeling cold.

An old family archives photograph of what I think must be Peace Celebrations in Blackburn. The crowds are vast. My father, who loved a throng of people, is amongst them. Note the men who are standing on the roof of Bradley's. When an empty Zeppelin passed over Stacksteads during World War I in 1916 my father with his cousin Sam Lord climbed through the fanlight and watched it from the roof—no mean feat when I recall father had only one good leg. The other was crippled by what was then known as Infantile Paralysis.

May Day revels were dying out when we were little. A survival of the festival in honour of the goddess of Spring and in rejoicing that the rigours of Winter were over, after hundreds of years' practice came down to our street in the shape of torn, old lace curtains, wooden, half hoops decorated with paper flowers, scraps of satin ribbon, whatever the mothers could rustle up in those hard times, but to us children they were gorgeous trappings. Imagination went a long way. We sang lustily about "crowning the Queen of the May" and even the boys joined in, blacking their faces and becoming "coconut men". Although I didn't know it, in ages past our village had been renowned for its "bringing in the May" and for the care put into it.

The coming of Spring still had great significance. Friends

"Gentle Nora Griffiths", a sworn enemy of ours, "up the Back", was crowned Queen of the May one year under half a wooden hoop trimmed with paper flowers. Her veil was a torn lace curtain. More paper roses nestled in her ginger hair and the floor-length skirt was an adapted damask table cloth. Of course we had a Maypole for real occasions, but a street lamp could always serve as makeshift.

and relatives flocked into town on a day of rejoicing and reunion. Easter Monday meant a trek up Holcombe Hill and some pace egging, which people must have done for "donkeys' years". It was something to look forward to. Nowadays families go off in the car as on any old weekend.

People were then still very superstitious. I remember being shocked when told that on no account must I take a twig of sweetly-smelling hawthorn into the house or it would cause my mother to die. Planned in my childish way as a lovely surprise, you may guess my feelings when it so miserably backfired. Some of the superstitions went back to pagan times. "The cat is raising the wind," said Grandmother, when Tiger tore at the furniture with his claws. If a cat died in the house that was bad luck, but if a black kitten

Every Easter Monday we climbed Holcombe Hill along with legions of other people, clutching packets of sandwiches and pop bottles, indulging in the rustic tradition. Once on top, we went up Peel Tower and neighbouring Grant's Tower until the latter became very dangerous and the public were warned off.

walked in that was good luck. As we had three cats there was a good chance of either. Amongst these wiseacre sayings, weather figured largely:

> *"If Rivington Pike do wear a hood,*
> *Be sure the day will ne'er be good."*

and

> *"When Pendle wears its woolly cap,*
> *The farmers all may take a nap."*

We found most true the following:

> *"When clouds appear like rocks and towers,*
> *The earth's refreshed by constant showers."*

Our prayers always finished with the verse we were taught to say, at that point. I have since found out that it was common practice in many parts of Lancashire and no doubt mother herself, grandmother and great-grandmother had all been taught like-wise. So much was passed on from mother to daughter, father to son.

"Matthew, Mark, Luke and John,
Bless the bed that I lie on."

An exciting spectacle for us in Summer was to watch the rooks flying overhead at sunrise to their rookery at the Grand Lodge. There were hundreds of them that appeared at a given time, darkening the sky, and it took many minutes for the flock to pass over. One day Edward brought a raven home. It had an injured wing. He, who loved all birds and living creatures, had found it at the foot of a tree after a spell of wild, windy weather. It perched on his shoulder, black, sinister-looking, with its long, sharp, yellow beak close to his face. He and the bird trusted each other implicitly and were quite relaxed, but my parents were afraid and insisted Edward take it back to the foot of the same tree. It must have broken Edward's heart to walk all that way back and abandon it, but he obeyed.

Cock fighting was officially a thing of the past, but father told stories about great-grandfather's visits to Kersal Moor where in the 18th century there was even a Ladies' Stand on

Edward, the eldest, "went for a soldier" as soon as World War II was declared in 1939. He had been hankering to set off for the Spanish Civil War. A young man full of ideals and old-fashioned chivalry, he soon became disenchanted but retained his love of birds and animals to the end. Lecturer at a Military College of Science and later employed at the Radar Research Establishment, Malvern, Edward specialised on Birdstrike *which minimised hazard to aircraft from flocks of birds. He wrote a paper for the magazine* Nature *on the subject.*

the race course. A cock-match between the gentlemen of Yorkshire and the gentlemen of Lancashire was held after the racing.

We had day trips to Blackpool and to Southport where Grandma Houghton, by now a very old lady, had retired. I remember the diamond-patterned tiles of Saunders Street and the first bag of shrimps I ever tasted at Southport: tangy, savoury, overhung with the salt scent of the sea. We also loved trips to the markets of Bury; Burnley, Chorley, Prestwich, Accrington, where I recall the pungent scent of celery hearts and displays of sausages and black puddings.

Father being a travelling photographer, meant we did get around. For a time he had a photographic studio at Waterfoot, close to Lewis Nuttall's shop. Carved chairs with barley-sugar shaped spindle backs gravitated from there to the spartan two up, two down cottage where we lived, an unusual mix with scrubbed linoleum, scrubbed table top and

The best thing about Southport Pier was the long ride to the end on a train which had real railway carriages. As a small child I recall the terror of going down the iron steps with the sea raging underneath. When we got to the end of the pier Grandma always wanted the loo and mother and I had to escort her.

53

Delivering fruit to Southport Market. On Saturday evenings, as markets closed "dinged" or damaged fruit could be bought very cheaply as otherwise over the weekend it grew mouldy and became useless. All kinds of fruit— redcurrants, blackcurrants, bilberries—were made into delicious pies for Sunday dinner. Especially I recall the purple bilberries when we four children grinned at each other like chows.

Great Uncle Jonathan's oil paintings on the walls. There were other small items of beauty amongst the stone jam jars pressed into service for containers and these made a difference to our lives, enriching the commonplace. I recall delicious Sunday lunches in early Spring, with a bunch of paper-white, scented narcissus on the table and a delicate, blue, glass water jug embossed with white marguerites.

Best of all we loved the country, walking on the Pennine hills, going "over the tops" from Edenfield and dropping down into Rossendale Valley, climbing from Downham, following the old Roman Road beyond Holcombe or questing around Clitheroe Castle and Whalley Abbey. Our first

Market Place, Heywood. "Bradleys the great clothiers" had a branch at Heywood, shown here c.1908 near the old Queen Anne Inn and the Golden Boot. The Queen Anne still had its resplendent, large inn sign. Opposite was Jackson's, long-established premises. Note the antique wall lamp. The trams made a thunderous approach at this curve but were quieter when this photograph was taken at twenty five minutes to five on an afternoon some ninety years ago.

Pendle Hill and Downham. "Here to the bone are my beginnings." To this day the area reeks of the true Lancashire heartland and I love it. I remember it in all weathers: shrouded in Autumn mist; etched clear against the sky in Summer; its great bluff shouldering starkly in icy Winter just before all-enveloping fog hid it from sight. The Lancashire Witches added nothing for me. Great Pendle always spoke for itself.

55

Albert Lee, the brave boy drowned in the River Roach, Heywood in making an heroic attempt to rescue his friend, hit local headlines on June 15th, 1907. Father was taking photographs there and it became one of his stories along with "Bill's O' Jack"s" and "Tom O" Bill's" of Greenfield. "Such interest did their tragic end excite, that 'ere they were removed from human sight, thousands on thousands daily came to see..." Many postcards in remembrance were printed by Bell of Heywood and A. and H. Hanson of Greenfield.

kingfisher was seen by the bridge at Dunsop, a never-to-be-forgotten streak of fire and sapphire against the rich, brown, wet earthiness of the river bank, where we also watched water boatmen skimming the surface, mayflies, dragonflies and in the shallows, paddling in our bare feet, constructed dams out of the clay.

All this seasonal activity seemed to work up to the most exciting time of all — Christmas, with its free shows in the shops.

On Christmas Show Night shopkeepers vied with each other to make the mouth water. Fish, geese, turkeys, ducks, rabbits, hares and all kinds of game and venison crammed the most up-to-date premises in town, but I hated to see the scrubbed, pink pigs so dead with big oranges popped into their gaping mouths, sometimes from which rolled a thin trickle of blood. Grapes arrived in barrels of cork in those days, the proud boast being "no foreign produce sold here". I liked the chemist's shop with its three enormous Winches-

In Christmas week, when I was a child, all the butchers' shops went mad, crowding their windows with sausages, hares and rabbits, but pride of place went centrally to a group of sprawling pigs, each with an orange in its mouth. Above them hung scores of chickens, ducks and turkeys. We loved Christmas dinner but the Christmas Show always uncomfortably put me off.

ter bottles of coloured liquids glowing blue, red and yellow alongside a huge pestle and mortar.

We gazed long and big-eyed at the toyshop windows in Manchester, knowing full well we would never see such magnificence in our home at Christmas. Well, a cat could look at a king!

CHAPTER 4

Station in Life

I REMEMBER watching from the wall a line of railway coaches stretching to below where I stood and under the bridge and beyond, and the last coach had not emerged from the tunnel at the further end of the platform. Hundreds of figures in khaki loaded with personal baggage, standing in groups, and the long, long time the train took to move off from the empty platform, for by then the men had gone. I remember being told that a famous locomotive, "The Great Bear", might pass by on that line — though now I think such an event would have been unlikely — and the keen disappointment I felt when it failed to appear. The General Strike was an interesting time when the railwaymen joined the miners to protest against cuts in wages that the government was forcing upon these workers. No proper trains ran for some days. True, an unexpected locomotive or two appeared on the line through long intervals of time, but there seemed to be a certain lack of expertise on the part of the driving staff, made up, I believe, of black-leg labour drawn from engineering students at the local university. The boilers ran out of steam frequently and firing was amateurish and consequently time-tables could by no means be relied upon, nor could the service. What I did notice was the long time the signal lamps remained alight with no attention, never had they been left so long unattended, and the reader must understand that signal lights were never extinguished apart from the brief time needed to trim and refill with oil.

Cleveleys Station. Holidays at Blackpool when the Illuminations were on came round annually and we had trips out to Cleveleys and Fleetwood. This station, which used to be full of Rossall Schoolboys, has now gone.

Beneath our kitchen window stood the platelayer's hut, where in foggy weather detonators placed on the up line before the passage of each train, exploded at regular time-intervals, and depending on the foulness of the fog the resultant sound varied from a resounding bang to a muffled bump. In the insalubrious atmosphere of freezing cold, sometimes with snow, and sulphurous mustard yellow smog, the platelayer at his brazier kept his vigil, a dim shadow behind the ruby glow of burning coke, whilst water distilled in drops on each piece of ice-cold metal exposed to the open air. Noisome air swirled around, irritating mucous membranes of nose and throat, and tiring pink-rimmed eyes, The fog forced its way into buildings everywhere, especially where the temperature was low, but even into dwelling houses it insinuated by way of ill-fitting doors and windows, rotting the Nottingham lace curtains and causing them to give off an odour of ammonia on washday as they sank beneath the thrice-renewed soapsuds.

But oh the Porters' Room on late Friday afternoons! Spit and polish in whitewood tabletop and the wooden forms drawn up alongside, all scrubbed like a butcher's counter. Concrete floor swabbed with very hot, soapy water strongly laced with tar oil disinfectant, and the step and fire surround tinted with cream donkey stone, fire range newly blackleaded with highlights of polished steel. The windows were freshly washed and polished and the opal glass lampshades. And such a delicious smell from the fire oven of baked potatoes, or the occasional warming-up of a recently-cooked meal waiting for some guard who intended to finish his shift at that station. As the evening advanced a pair of oil hand lamps were lit and stood in a prominent place, and the coal scuttle, topped up with best coal from the bunker outside, was brought in and placed near the fire. Two single rings on the bell — that's the signalman — take his can of water before dusk and then we are ready for the evening and the longer waits between trains.

Our station received parcels but had no goods yard; nothing larger than a basket of racing pigeons or a milk churn was accepted there, though the station at the village next along boasted its coal yard with bays, goods warehouse, loading gauge and stationary crane with wooden jib which never seemed to be put to use. It also had a passenger siding referred to as 'The Bay', and from which vantage point one could watch the local cricket team play in Summer without payment.

To where was the rolling stock of those days finally shunted? Where did it terminate its working life? First, the wooden coal trucks, ten or twelve tons capacity, with manually-applied brakes, most of them seemingly to have seen their last coat of paint decades before my time. The name of each coal company was painted on each wagon: 'Butterly', read one, 'Staveley', another. There were so many names and there were the other purpose-built trucks or vans, fish or fruit, or double length wooden louvered milk vans from Scotland. Then those proprietary vans: 'Colmans' or 'Cerebos', and later 'Fyffes', each designed for the job in hand.

I wonder how many different designs of guard's van existed in the days of steam? There seemed to be so many variations on the single theme: some squat with an open platform at one end and running on two pairs of wheels and some longer ones mounted on three pairs of wheels. All, however, had that indispensable chimney protruding through the roof, more often than not with a thin wisp of blue smoke trailing behind. Each side of the van, too, had observation slits with glass panes through which the guard could watch front and rear of the train. There was a time when I envied the goods guard, for he must have been a fortunate man with no passengers to chivvy on the train nor wellwishers to warn away from the platform edge; no mailbags to hinder his time schedule nor packages to delay his passage. He had not even the easy task of ejecting a bundle of town newspapers onto a country platform. He was utterly dependent on the driver for the speed of the goods he carried and on the acumen of the signalman for the alacrity of his passing from section to section (bearing in mind also the regulations of the railway company). What did this most fortunate man do to while away the time? Obviously he must have stood against the steel bar barrier outside his cabin, watching the scenery pass between straight track and curve, cutting and embankment, incline and descent, girder bridge, tunnel and brick viaduct as the locomotive puffed steadily on its way mile after mile. When this palled, or when he was hungry or the weather was wet or otherwise inclement, or when night had fallen, he betook him to the glowing stove within, to refuel and warm himself or to cook thereon an abundance of sizzling gammon rashers, lying alongside a couple of orange-yoked eggs and brown fingers of fried bread. Later a pint pot or two of hot, sweet tea and a following pipe of fragrant tobacco. Beyond lighting his lamp what else could he have had to do?

And our station nowadays? "Passengers must not cross the line except by the bridge," the original notice still reads. It is one of the few things that have not altered in all these years, when so much else has. Crossing that bridge I look down on the carriage roof on which infinitesimal fragments of steel thrown off by friction between high tension cable and pantograph have oxidised in the rain. Driblets of water blown into crazy patterns at high speed stagger along, rusty brown, to the rear. The sound of motion is different: there's no longer the endless deh-deh, deh-dey—de-deh, deh-dey—deh-deh, deh-deh to lull one into a state of quiescence. Never again will we hear the comforting rhythm of the wheels as they traverse the lengths of steel track for nowadays rails are continuous strips of steel. No longer is there a leather strap to release a window to absorb the smell of burning coal from the engine, for warm and well-lit carriages now cosset us from the elements outside.

CHAPTER 5

Trial by Gaslight

*A vivid portrayal of Schooldays emerges from my brother
Charles's recollections.*

ACROSS the street from Big Croft was the school. The
Senior part was nearest the lower playground, and the
Infants above the Three Steps in a more-restricted space.
Some of my earliest memories stem from here. There was
the Kindergarten schoolroom with its cheerful fire in
Winter, protected by a big, brass-railed fireguard. Here the
alphabet was held aloft in the monitor's hand, letter following letter in the usual sequence and repeated by the little
ones until known. Even now I can remember the rectangles
of pink card with the letter complete with serifs in indian
ink. Here, too, were the little tables and chairs and the rocking horse that was purchased the term we left the room so
that we never had a ride. Bowls of bulbs in Spring brightened the surroundings and here was the reed organ for
sustaining infant voices of indeterminate pitch, one of
which I still recall

> Come, little leaves," said the wind one day,
> Come o'er the meadows with me, and play;
> Put on your dresses of red and gold;
> Summer is gone, and the days grow cold.

and now another one has come to mind

Master North Wind's blowing, Ooooh...
Through the forest he is going, Ooooh...
Can't you hear his voice so shrill,
Can't you hear him whistle still,
Master North Wind's blowing, Oooo...

The teacher wore a blouse and a long, certainly well below the knee, skirt in Donegal tweed and a large wristlet watch, leather encased, which she told us once belonged to her brother who had died not that many years before in the trenches of Flanders. From here we went to the second class in the Big Room with its painted brick walls. From the wooden skirting was three feet of dark green gloss, two inches of black and to the ceiling the rest in light cream gloss. There was plaster only on the ceiling and tiles were non-existent, and I think I am right in saying that the walls were repainted every three years.

In this second class with its four sides of blanket stitch round a rectangle of dark blue paper, with its raffia teapot stands and the initiation into those mysterious 'tables' we had heard so much about we were also introduced to drawing. We began by making a drawing of the teacher's smart red handbag and the desks ran scarlet that day. We sat at two-seater desks which had slate slots, though slates were before my time, and almost every subject was performed in them except a species of simple, unexciting P.E., without apparatus, called "Drill". Our hand work now included hair tidies "to hang on mother's dressing table", and the beginning of paper models planned from the flat. Whenever bored, and there **were** times, one tried to relieve the monotony by glancing round the walls at the framed illustrations from Barrie's Peter Pan by Mabel Lucy Attwell, or cogitating on the framed presentation shield hung above the central fireplace. We were not told a single fact about it, so we simply took it for granted and made no effort to find out.

And so to Junior class one, though the notice, cloth on rollers, said Regulations of the Public Elementary School, or some such.

Junior class one was in Lower School below Three Steps and the lower playground. This part of the school was in charge of a headmaster. There we saw him but a few months — and then no more. That a child should die, through the chances and hazards we knew. One of the better-dressed boys in my class, he wore brown wellingtons (which were then, I think, a new idea for children) had to come daily over the fields which were often wet in Winter and had the misfortune to catch meningitis. Later we were told he had died. About the same time that Winter another, poorer boy caught diphtheria, quite common then, with its companion Scarlet Fever, and he too, succumbed. For a teacher to cease suddenly to be in school when we were not told that he had left to take another job seemed awfully strange and something to wonder at. Then we were told that he had died suddenly. Later we were asked to contribute a copper or two as a school gesture to a memorial wreath. Later still, the older pupils were led to the graveyard half a mile away to view the red granite memorial stone that had been erected over his grave.

In the short time I saw this headmaster, I was quite overawed. He was one of the old fashioned type in which **all** material should, if possible, be turned into an example or lesson somewhat on the Chinese idea that one picture is worth a thousand words. His class and school discipline was wonderful to behold; he had but to turn his head to any direction for silence to fall **immediately**. I rather doubt if he ever was an approachable person—he was the essence of Victorian authority.

The week I moved to the Lower School, a boy who had stepped out of line, was to be shown the error of his ways, not merely corrected or summarily punished by caning, but

65

brought before the whole school and there displayed as the "awful example" from which we must ever flee. It seemed to be more of an exercise, less of a punitive retribution than a re-enactment of the way the dread law dealt with condemned criminals in Newgate in the eighteenth and early nineteenth centuries. Let us remember that it was rare for a child raised during the second half of Victoria's reign to be allowed the **slightest** deviation from the path laid out for it: bear in mind that the only book usually allowed for the child's reading on Sundays, apart from the Bible and assuming he was not a Roman Catholic, was that grim horror *Foxe's Book of Martyrs*, illustrated. To continue: a bell rang fifteen minutes before the end of afternoon school and one by one in silence classes marched into the Hall, there to stand erect in columns before the small platform, which was to do duty as a 'scaffold'. The teachers neatly arranged themselves round the wall and a senior boy lit the gas lamps (since, it being late December the room was now becoming dark), which he did with a taper affixed to a map pole. The 'malefactor', rather than naughty child, entered immediately followed by the headmaster and in that order they mounted the place of 'execution'. The closing hymn of the day was announced, and from memory the children sang, verses five and six being appropriate to the crime committed

> *When deep within our swelling hearts*
> *The thoughts of pride and anger rise,*
> *When bitter words are on our tongues,*
> *And tears of passion in our eyes;*
>
> *Then we may stay the angry blow*
> *Then we may check the hasty word,*
> *Give gentle answers back again,*
> *And fight a battle for our Lord.*

All this time the condemned stood alone at one end of

the platform with lowered head and dejected mien whilst justice in bald head, walrus moustache, winged collar and pince-nez stood at the other. The hymn finishing and the closing prayer read an anticipatory silence fell as the head-master advanced to the small table and faced the school with his right forefinger resting on the table edge. He sternly read the indictment and by stressing the seriousness of the misdemeanour and sentence being pronounced, the children, if possible grew more quiet than ever. "Come here, boy: hold out your right hand." The boy faltered and then advanced, and the cane discreetly hidden by the table was now raised to full view. He flinched as the first blow struck but dumbly carried out instruction as the headmaster conti-nued, "And now the other hand." For full theatrical effect it would have been better with muffled drums but the dra-matic silence, now broken by cries from the weeping child caused the young audience to glance with horror at the Jack Ketch standing above his victim. The master went on, "And now turn your face to the wall: your name will be written in the Black Book." In silence we were dismissed. Let us there-fore, move over to my class.

In this class for the one and only time at school I was teacher's blue-eyed pupil—I simply couldn't go wrong, ex-cept once! On that occasion I was beaten by a boy I had never considered a rival. He was Cecil, yes Cecil, and he was blonde, slim, spoke well, had clean buffed nails and impeccable manners. In comparison I was a non-starter. In addition to his pious appearance he would think nothing, if the teacher suggested it, of singing the alternate verses of 'The Keys of Canterbury' whilst facing a girl of the class who sang the other verses. Worse still, he would with his left arm raised and right palm pressed to his heart, kneel before the blushing damsel and sing in his clear treble that he would give the keys of his heart and be married till death do us part . . . Which girl partner didn't seem to matter one iota; had I been vigorously pushed and my arm well twisted I perhaps, would have considered singing a verse or two to Freda, who had shining brown bobbed hair, freckles and dimples and always a lovely smile, but not kneeling. Perhaps even Bernice of the heart shaped face and springy auburn curls, too, but Cecil would elegantly genuflect whichever girl stood before him, and without any prompting, showed no partisan feeling in the matter. My position sank still lower when he freely volunteered to sing at an Open Day a sentimental and high toned ditty called My Task, that repeated the strain, And Smile When Evening Falls, in a most convincing rendition, whilst looking up to Heaven like the picture of an Italian saint in a Catholic repository. He left school soon afterwards and no one took his place. When Cecil left I was free again to continue my course without rivalry: seldom did I fall below the top of the class in the weekly tests, for I led in Arithmetic and practically everything else. I served my teacher with complete devotion—even now with so many years past I consider her a great teacher. She certainly knew how to get me to work.

Pride goeth . . . in the next class I fell from grace. I could not appreciate the dry wit of the middle-aged spinster in charge. Contrariwise, my brother got on like a house on fire and did very well. Only in one thing did I make good progress in her class, and it was something not taught in the school — I became acting (unpaid) school pianist for I was better at playing piano than any of the teaching staff, but that wasn't saying a great deal. One thing she did teach me and most of the other children was singing from Tonic Solfa, eventually from sight, an accomplishment that is not strong in British schools nor has been for forty years or more, and that was no small thing, speaking as a musician.

Parish pump patriotism was still in full spate in school, even so soon after the "war to end all wars", and it was poured over us by the panful, in History, in Poetry and in Song. There seemed to be no end to it: There's a Land a Dear Land; Three Cheers for the Red, White and Blue; Ye Mariners of England; Hearts of Oak; Kipling's Recessional, Land of our Birth; Our England is a Garden; If; and Puck of Pook's Hill; The Arethusa together with the inescapable Land of Hope and Glory and great dollops of Sir Henry Newbolt and like-minded poets.

It was a common act for the whole school to parade in the playground and for the boys to March Past and Salute the Flag on Empire Day, marching by in twos and forming fours for inspection. When one schoolgirl wrote an essay "Why I am Proud to be British" or some such in rather jingoistic terms and had been gently criticised by a visiting H.M. Inspector with broader views , the partisan *Daily Mail* sold many more copies with their write up on the case.

And so to the last teacher of that school, the headmaster himself, not the one of my earlier years but a younger man who also lived with his cane within easy reach, and more uncertain in its use! He took a divided class: the greater part of whom intended to leave at the age of fourteen, and a tiny set being coached for the few county scholarships in the county with the largest population. I was in the latter section. Each day invariably began with headmaster taking down a cane — it was kept hanging on a prominent place on the wall — and with it he would flail the nearest desk crying: "Fireworks, that's what we're going to have today. And a free show of fireworks for all who haven't remembered." I would look through the high class room windows, gently moving my head from left to right to see the house chimneys opposite ripple like a belly dancer through the inequalities in the glass. Barbara hid her confused mind in a useless ploy that all her classmates knew was unavailing — she developed a shocking cough within seconds of the lesson beginning. Then there was Annie. She was, without doubt, Deirdre of the Sorrows and

69

daily entered school weeping, being daily thirty minutes late, carrying in her relaxed hand some pathetic floral tribute to the teacher, be it buttercups and daisies or daffodils. Auburn haired, feckless Annie, Heaven only knows why she came to our school since she was very Irish and a Roman Catholic. "Indian wives resort to suttee in their country on the deaths of their husbands. Why, and who stamped out suttee in India?" The small, usual, band of 'didn't know' began to wend its way to the front of the class, hands at the ready — to be caned! You've done it before and you'll do it again, so why bother; let's get it over; you can't win in this game. The cliches and the conjecture without a shred of foundation and the claptrap surmise rapidly gleaned from the "popular" press, how often did we hear it? The personal likes and dislikes; the unsubstantiated newspaper reportage and real facts thrown out together, pure water polluted by seepage from a less-wholesome source. Scepticism developed. There was not much enjoyment here as far as I found myself and at last when I gained a county scholarship I left with no regrets.

CHAPTER 6

Tom Mix and
The Art Gallery

WHILST I was a girl, the cinema or kinema as Arthur Mee (editor of the long defunct Children's Newspaper and Children's Pictorial, would have it, was growing in popularity. These grand halls of rich magnificence and most doubtful architectural pedigree were springing up all over the land offering two-and-a-half hours of dream-world entertainment at low cost. Because of the last consideration we attended perhaps once a fortnight in our most enamoured period, and thereafter as the years passed, we went less and less until it became an occasional change in the way we spent our leisure time.

Even the way to the local picture house could, or perhaps one day would, lead to adventure, or so we often hoped! Skirting the steam laundry where the gas engine blasted its exhaust beneath a double layer of corrugated iron sheeting and shaking the immediate earth as we passed down the bank, we advanced along the sandy track suitable only for children since there were two four foot fences to climb before the Brow (pronounced Brew). Alongside the stream issuing from a railway cutting culvert flooded in heavy down-pour, the path continued over a clapper bridge of gritstone and alongside the blue painted palings to a leafy, country lane. Then the dingle, site of the old Rectory in the fifteenth and sixteenth centuries, where golden fluffy male

I believe these girls were all sisters or at least related. Trained by Beryl Gibbs, they came from London to the Palace at Manchester and I thought them very talented, but our greatest treat was to see Curigwen Lewis as Alice in Wonderland and later a production of Peter Pan at the same theatre. On the way home mother bought us the books from Sherratt and Hughes, which made the treat perfect.

flowers of Great Sallow smoked yellow pollen as one brushed by them about Eastertide. There was also an ancient draw well where we would often sit round the edge fully ten feet in diameter, dangling our bare knees (boys don't seem to have knees nowadays; they are always shielded from the elements by cloth). Mercifully the well was dry and about four feet deep, for none of us could swim. Beyond was "no man's pasture" where a ragged and dishevelled man existed in a hovel of random planks, sacking, old tarpaulin and beaten iron sheeting. With him dwelt his rough pelted horse and neither seemed to work in the way society expects. We called him The Hermit. He didn't encourage visitors, especially children. Only one big field to pass through, where the annual circus rested, directed by Lord John Sanger and supporting the usual lions and tigers and an inordinate number of elephants, or so it seemed to me. Then at last, our goal, the Picturedrome. The entrance fee for one child to the first house was 2d and with an added $^1/2$d penny one could buy a stick of Everton toffee and make it a night out.

I cannot hope to enumerate and name all, or even a tiny fraction of those silent cinematograph shows we sat through, but they may yet appear on television. Tom Mix the cowboy was one of our heroes, although, shameful of me, I have forgotten the name of his faithful steed. The name Starlight hovers around. Buster Keaton and Harold Lloyd amused; Lon Chaney terrified; Douglas Fairbanks thrilled, especially in films like 'The Mark of Zorro'. Films like Conrad's 'Nostromo'; Wilder's 'The Bridge of San Luis Rey'; Blasco-Ibanez' 'The Four Horsemen of the Apocalypse' or any of Maugham's filmed novels appealed because of their action; the psychological patterns were quite lost on us. Gorky's 'Mother' was a film like no other. Its real people (rather than paper figures) saddened; its gloom and grey drabness appalled and long it stayed in my memory.

'Belphagor' was a weekly cliff-hanger as was also 'The Iron Maiden' and those repetitive Sax Rohmer Dr. Fu Manchu series that lasted week after week, month after month, until one stayed away for sheer boredom. We saw several versions of 'A Yankee at King Arthur's Court' — the Will Rogers one was the best, I thought, and the mechanised steeds contributed by the Yankee in the earliest version. Motor cycles, had developed into Austin Sevens in the last. 'The Hunchback of Notre Dame' and 'Beau Geste' also were directed more than once.

There was another cinema two miles along the road known amongst the coarser rustics and vulgar little boys as "The Fleapit" or "Bughouse". It was a noisy place and the clientele was not so select as in the Picturedrome. True, one could gain entrance to a Saturday matinee in the first five rows of seats for as little as one penny, old coinage, but throughout the performance there could be a shower of orange peel falling on the righteous and unrighteous alike and we were strongly discouraged by our parents from attending, or, if we did then we dare not complain. We did go, and thus had a penny left over to buy a bottle of 'pop' with a black vulcanite screw stopper. Dearer mineral water cost about 3d. and had to be shared since its exorbitant cost ruled out one apiece. These superior bottles had a dimpled neck and the pressure of the gas within was held by a glass marble. This pressure was overcome by forcing the "alley" to the middle of the neck and so permitting gas to escape together with the beverage. Oh, the dandelion and burdock, the American ice cream soda, the lemonade, we consumed! Eventually we forsook those coloured, flavoured and sweetened powders, euphemistically called Lemonade and Raspberryade. Even with dilution I never liked them, nor, for that matter, was I wildly enthusiastic about kali or sherbet powder. Some children took tiger nuts and liquorice root to chew, but they were hard to come by in our area. Peanuts (ex-shells) were "coming-in" then, and monkey nuts became more scarce.

Now and again we would travel to the further cinema by tram, and that meant no sweets or pop. Two nearby towns used electricity for their transport on the two main roads, chiefly tramcars, though there were a few electric trolley buses, which were still a novelty and none came anywhere near our village. The smaller town, less affluent, had a route passing The Street and Butterthorn Lane and this was the one we used. The bigger town, which was more important, and richer, could use trams of the largest size, indeed they were the largest I saw anywhere. They had four wheel bogies at the front and the rear, instead of the usual four spaced wheels, and had also in consequence a smoother ride. They were totally enclosed from the weather, had upholstered seats downstairs and passed magnificently down the thoroughfare looking like nothing less than gigantic illuminated glass panelled display cabinets. Moreover, each tram had a trolley boy, in addition to the two man team of driver and conductor. To the simple onlooker the job of trolley boy, a trainee youth, seemed to consist chiefly of moving the trailing power pole to the rear of the vehicle when either terminus was reached. On the other hand "our trams" were more primitive, had holed birchwood seats in light yellow stain downstairs and slatted seats on the "top deck". I purposely say 'top deck' since it was named that

The open-top, double-deck Preston tram symbolises their widespread general usefulness throughout Lancashire. Small wonder these gliding monsters have passed into the folklore. They were a splendid means of reaching theatre or the "silent films". The latter cost threepence on the front row, but soon came the "Talkies". I used to get so carried away by such adventure films as Conquest, my brothers found me a great embarrassment but I could not go without them.

75

and also because it could be like travelling on the top deck of a small coaster in a choppy sea. It was a copy of the Big Dipper in an amusement fair as swinging sideways, bounding and swaying up and down on miles of roads metalled in granite setts, whilst the wind and rain (in OUR tram there was no roof at all on the top deck) ruffled the hair and the water fell on the deck and drained away into the lee or starboard scuppers, accompanied by the screams and hum of the trolley pulley, with blinding and crackling flashes lighting up the roadside (especially after dark) between pulley and high- tension wire. With every bend or turn at speed the wheels, influenced by the road's camber, smote with their rims against the grooved rails and hummed and rang like chinese gongs. It sounds exciting: we thought it was, and all for one penny. At a crossroads or obstructing vehicle or anything similar that delayed progress the driver would clang his resonant deep-toned bell. Some driving cabs were even more primitive than ours and had no enclosing screen for the driver and there he stood in heavy black rainwear and flat uniform cap covered against wet with a mackintosh cover gathered with elastic, shod in heavy boots or wellingtons, and peering over the metal waist high surround centred by the headlight for hazards ahead. In fog he was quite dependent on the driver ahead since it was impossible for him to overtake, and huge traffic jams built up at an amazing speed. The conductor who accepted fares carried a variety of tickets of differing colours, uses and charges, which were printed in thin card, and ingeniously carried around clipped to a wood and metal frame and hanging from the left wrist by a leather strap. An issued ticket was musically punched like the bell on a typewriter by a cancelling machine, which the conductor carried around with him.

* * * *

There was another art-form besides films that one could

indulge in free, and I certainly indulged and it was painting. A small, provincial art gallery housed in a medium-
sized and classically designed country house and
surrounded by almost a thousand acres of parkland lay one
mile from where I lived. Admission was daily and free;
consequently we went there often to watch and observe.
Perhaps I was a little surprised that the late occupants —the
house now belonged to a nearby city—had lived in such
style and surroundings. Even the story of Cinderella had
not prepared me for this, and the possibility of having spa-
ciousness, quality and beauty around one instead of the
cramped utilitarianism and basic shelter of an artisan's
dwelling of two up and two down came as a mild shock.
Entering the house multiple pairs of doors in figured Spanish mahogany with ormulu furniture and elaborate plaster
jambs and architraves opening on most rooms drew my
attention and admiration. A wide, shallow stepped staircase rose from a marble-pillared hall; painted and gilded
cast iron lamp posts elegantly mounted on tripods and surrounded with simple and tasteful glass lanterns caught my
attention: how splendid to be thus lighted to bed instead of
a naked batswing jet on a plain gas pipe, I decided, and on
the floor lavishly polished wood. My lady's circular bou-
doir, surrounded by a dozen, spaced cheval glasses, was
something to see again and again, but most of all I wanted
the pictures, English water colours, they drew me like a
magnet more than anything else there.

In time I learned to some degree to recognise the style of
David Cox, some of whose paintings seemed, unlike most
water colours, quite large. Only Samuel Prout appeared to
turn out paintings of like size but Prout's paper was whiter
and smoother—at times I was sure I could recognise tiny fragments of straw in the rough, grey or off white paper Cox used.
There were other differences too. Cox was a man of the wind
and the rain, whether on the sea or, more commonly, in hilly

country, often Wales, and the trees, the rocks, the sheep and
the human figures knew the elements and lived in them. His
subdued blues and sepias that enhanced the distances in his
work were in marked constrast to the milder pastel shades of
Prout. Another thing, Prout used town scenes, and churches,
ancient and historical buildings inhabited by many more humans with carts and coaches, 'diligences' they were called,
moving in and out of the streets. His colours, like Copley
Fielden's, had choice, wider and more liberal colour selection
and his skies seemed set for fair weather. Fielden's were small
pictures of meticulous draughtsmanship not a bit like David
Cox's bustling with enormous energy. Fielden's were exqui-
sitely tinted and more like Thomas Girtin's, though the latter
artist used a more limited palette. His work, Girtin's, pleased
me immensely. There weren't enough of his to compare —
and the way to paint was floated on paper, especially in the
painting of a Cistercian abbey in the north. Others that appealed were Paul de Loutherbourg, Peter de Wint and the
Varley brothers. Not all the pictures took my fancy: there was
an oil by Turner which ran with colour. It seemed as if the
artist had applied a fully loaded brush and without brushing
out the paint, left it to run down the canvas in thin runnels,
nor had ever returned to the work. Other oil colours by John
Linnell, by Richard Wilson I did like and a most realistic English country scene with cattle by William Shayer, but on the
whole, probably because of their size I was better able to enjoy
the water colours. No doubt nowadays, schoolchildren are
regularly instructed in art in galleries and the things to look
for and appreciate fully explained, but I had to find my own
way, limited though it was and I am deeply grateful to the
City Fathers there who allowed me the run of the place.

CHAPTER 7

Adventures in Irwell Vale

HERE, ages ago, an ancient river flowed into a lake, and the rich deposited sediment it had brought now formed the level floor of the valley a mile wide and several miles long. Between that time and now the lake had disappeared and the river, still flowing, moved over to the right hand side above a fault in the strata, and through the long years had cut a sixty-foot ravine in the out-cropping rock. The valley width was the natural boundary between teeming town with its offensively noisy industry, sooty public buildings and seemingly-endless rows of back-to-back artisans' cottages and long gloomy streets of granite setts, and the rural parish adjoining, half buried in an undulating seclusion of fields, copses and little dells.

During the early railway age the iron way crept along valley sides parallel, sponsored by get-rich-quick promoters, but because of the geologcal fault only one stretch of line developed financially. This side passed pitheads and metal, coal and ceramic industries. The further side ran through quiet ways where the carboniferous strata lay too deep to exploit, and the land was extensively agricultural and thus its permanent way gathered and deposited little freight. Passengers also were few so that in time its five stations became two, mere halts embowered in greenery.

79

Soon after the second halt the railway turned right wheel and joined the busier line by means of a great viaduct. This viaduct built of blue engineering bricks thirteen arches long stretched across the valley floor at right angles to the river, crossing the stream in one effortless bound with a beautiful and larger seventh arch. The rocky banks on which the piers of this arch were placed furnished an anchor point for a stone abutment keyed into the living rock and projected into the stream like the salley of an ancient castle. The abutment deflected the scouring current, preventing the undermining of the pier on that side. Now the apex of the larger arch, that serene bow of many thousands of bricks, could not have been less than eighty feet above the water's surface, but higher still, rising above the parapet and its stone feather-edging, stood the signal box, at approximately mid-channel, with the signalman like a sea captain on a ship's bridge.

Along the ravine sides randomly-planted stands of hardwood trees struggled to survive in polluted air blowing from the factories, and toxic sulphur dioxide fumes claimed victims yearly, yet still Nature asserted herself to restore the balance. Oaks, sycamore and beech trees, beneath whose boughs wild hyacinths bloomed in Springtime seemed from the distance to rise from rich blue-misty fields, so thickly grew the flowers, and as the tree buds unfolded each tree could be recognised according to his kind, by the shade of green. The oaks were a mustard green, the green of parched peas that have been boiled too long; the sycamores were darker with a splash of burnt umber, and besides, the tree disposed its leaves in tiers like the tiers of a grand wedding cake and could thus otherwise be recognised. The beeches were of a stronger, darker green and towered above the other trees. Beneath them the shadows were very deep.

A matter of a furlong upstream and parallel to the viaduct, but much inferior to it in size and height, indeed only a little higher than the ravine sides, stood an aqueduct of yellow stone, and from which, randomly chosen by wind and suitable matrix, grew hardy ferns, sprouting bright fronds in the Summer months. The aqueduct carried a short section of one of the narrow broad canals that followed a low contour along the valley. From his elevated position the signalman could see the permanent way he controlled was in plan a duplication of the navigation of half a century earlier, and the three factories accordingly took advantage of both facilities, each establishment having its railway siding and canal wharf

Described in 1838 as "a valley rich with the choicest beauties of rural scenery which could scarcely be surpassed . . ." A little later the district had a famous Society of Botanists, working men all, and a local inn named after the new railway and the naturalists, in that order.

This place was so far from our homes that we visited it only when we had a full day to spare and could bring with us our sandwiches and bottles of fizzy drinks. Common sense kept us a stone's throw from the industry, for it was a noisome place and besides, there was always a labourer to question our approach and to threaten us, even with the canal between.

By the ceramic wharf, from a six inch drain a continuous stretch of milkiness, diluted slip seeping into the canal, created a cloudy, opaque stream where nothing ever grew, yet the steady flood of water in turn dissipated the whiteness and only a short distance further on water plantain and flags reappeared.

The next factory was offensive to nose, ears and eyes: drifting veils of exhausted boiler steam floated from many traps and pipes and in the moister air the nose became more susceptible to the ever-present stench. Sprawling heaps of burning vulcanite waste gave off dense, greasy black smoke in contrast to which that smoke from the bottle kilns seemed less offensive. There was an acridity of chlorine and a real or imagined taste of metal on the lips as one has after handling much copper coinage. Ears were assailed with the hammering of power presses and the clang, screech and screaming whine of metal meeting metal.

Here we crossed the humpback bridge and so up the pathway of small cobbles where the tow horse changed from one side to the other. Guarding it stood a massive eight-foot restraining post where the rope friction of almost a century and a half had gouged deep parallel channels to half the post's girth. We trailed our hands over marble-smooth stone parapets bound with iron straps, and stared down into the deeps of the water, continuing for a further mile to a disused spur of the canal where a graveyard of narrow boats, hulk after hulk, lay, fascinating, eerie and romantic.

Some boats showed only a prow and some a stern with or without a tiller and slanting heavy wooden rudder. Some showed all the upper work and some were still cargoed with empty coal tubs of robust timber construction, but each and every one holed below the water line. They bore no names — only the number the colliery had provided — whilst pond weed grew in them along with rushes and reed mace palisaded them round about. On the surface floated duckweed, a smothering blanket of minute, vivid green discs. Here in Summer brilliant and bronzed demoiselles in blue and green darted and hovered above the gaudy flags with their strap-like leaves and ramrod stiffness, and in late August the golden, gauzy-winged great dragon fly alternately clung to the leaf and patrolled up and down his territorial stretch.

This spur of the navigation ended at a small tower of dark red brickwork badly in need of pointing, about ten feet high, and crowned with a high railing of sharp iron spikes deeply pitted with rust. Into the base of the tower as into a vast mouth the canal overflowed, and by way of a shallow stone sill and wooden hatch, smoothly slid through an arch, heavily barred. Unseen but heard the waters disappeared into this well with a thrilling roar whilst at one corner a wayward water jet, spraying sideways continuously, soaked the fleshy, green liverwort spreading over the masonry there.

"Never watch running water in the mass" we had been advised many times, unless there is a railing in front of you, and so, fearfully turning away after the initial look, we moved away to other things.

Sooner or later we retraced our steps along the towing path, back over the yellow aqueduct and struck out across country to the quiet stretch of railway. Sometimes we followed field paths along hedges bright in April green leaf, disturbing unobtrusive dunnocks and chanting yellowhammers, whilst above us, the kestrels that nested in the put-log holes of the blue viaduct quartered the fields, hovering or gliding in short, rapid bursts of flight. A little earlier in the season it was the peewits who were most conspicuous in their fascinating behaviour. Over the meadows still bare after Winter ploughing the sadly complaining birds on broad rounded wings flew erratically in mock attack, dropping vertically, wings like slowly turning sycamore keys falling from the sky, effortlessly checking the dive and lifting again vigorously or wheeling hither and thither in marvellous aerobatics. Sometimes we stumbled on their nests rather than found them, shallow saucers of soil with two or three large eggs like the brown eggs of a domestic fowl strikingly blotched in dark chocolate.

Our passage when May and early June had come was hazarded by sappy grass, long and wet with heavy dew or recent shower and we were soon wet in our boots, quicker still if we wore shoes, for socks soaked immediately even though we skirted the ditches fringed with horsetail and bedecked with water crowfoot and cuckoo flower. Accordingly we changed our route overland and persisted down the lane poorly metalled in crusted furnace clinker and grey, dusty coke ash.

Whitsuntide was well past but the prevailing colour of the wild flowers was white, and week after week white persisted. There was the light cream of cow parsley dominating the verges, umbels and finely fretted foliage nodding in the gentle wind, and backing it white mayblossom flowering to capacity on every quickthorn hedge or isolated tree. Elder flowers with flattened panicles coloured deep cream as cauliflower curds and heavily scented. In the hedge bottoms, garlic mustard still lingered with glowing metallic- white flowers as though made of an oxide of zinc. Here, in the shadow of the wood could be detected a heavier, more pungent smell of garlic, the wild ramsons whose myriad heads as white as snowdrops stretched, thickly clustered, far away and out of view.

At the end of the lane at the further side of the valley an escarpment of pure sand rose above us the existence of which we or any other passers-by might well be unaware but for the betrayal of its golden hillocks by the rabbits, for their burrows showed up like the bunkers of a golf course, and elsewhere was a thin black topburden covered with young woodland, or a scant outcrop of red sandstone poking through the acid soil.

Along the escarpment at a suitable contour the single rail track edged along for several miles through small stands of oak, birch and hazel and past a pine tree or two whose positions had been determined by chance rather than by choice. From mid April onwards the song of the willow tit and chiff chaff were heard above the soft chuff-chuffing of the locomotive and through the lush growth of the later season on sunny days the carriages were dappled in light and shadow, whilst through half-opened windows rich odours of bark and leaf and flower slowly distilling their sweetness in the humid alembic of high Summer. The few travellers nodded and dozed in their pleasant indolence, overcome by the heat.

At the other side of the track along the course described lay a little dell, Fitch Holes, marked on the older maps but of such insignificance the railway builders threw a raised embankment at right angles to and across it, piercing the piled earth with a stone-faced culvert to allow natural springs and floodwater to drain away. Then they had forgotten it so that it remained secret and unknown to all but a few local folk. There were no paths there. Badgers had once occupied setts there, though not in living memory, but weasels could be seen, rarely, if one were fortunate to be there at the right time, and had a quick eye. Other small mammals roved its grassy floor, field mice commonly traversed it, and hedgehogs, and from time to time the body of the common shrew, that tiny animal with such an excitable temper and so many enemies, was found. This little area, difficult of access and hidden from many eyes, was our goal.

On once arriving we saw little cause to bustle along like the tiny brook sliding on its course along the valley floor, dropping in miniature cataracts over the sills and ledges of outcrop rock, or creeping under rank grasses or beneath the shadow of long bramble shoots where the half-buoyant water vole paddled, moving his blunt head from side to side searching for provender between the thick cresses. How pleasant it was to lie supine on sun warmed thymey turf below the heather bordering the valley side, and watch small copper butterflies busy on nettles and scabious heads and magenta thistles, the unheeded book (brought in the jacket pocket and meant to be read) lying open to the sky.

Thus the long Summer passed. The bracken that had grown

ever thicker and higher now lost its green resilience, stiffened with age and burned in the heat, but we had long returned to our classrooms before the heather flowers paled and the bramble fruits turned black. They, in turn, passed their peak of excellence as the blow flies sought them out, clinging, piercing and sucking until the fruits turned dull and unpleasant. Dog rose hips reddened and burnet rose hips became even more scarlet in the shrinking daylight hours of increasing coolness and brief evening gave place to night as the woodcock sought its roost amongst the hazel thicket and the owls began to call.

CHAPTER 8

Trouble at
th'mills

*The transition from childhood fascination to the harsh
reality of life emerges when Charles starts work.*

KEARSLEY'S mill lodge took the waters of the short,
precipitous stream, and this stream, fed by several
springs and field drains had its main source in a gentle
hillside, and forming a narrow defile or clough, descended
to the river meadows before falling into the main channel
below. In the stream's higher reaches, where a child could
stand astride its waters, the water mints grew thick, and
buttercups could always be found. Later these plants gave
way to wild garlic and meadowsweet, celandine, and
higher up, wood anemone and oxalis. A colony of indian
balsam had climbed from the river verge and moved upstream also, but owing to the exceeding wetness of the site
had taken no great hold thereon. Willows grew here in variety, and several alders. A wide meander, a low bank of
golden sand where the undermined roots of birch trees en-
tangled themselves and held back any immediate plant
growth, was a favourite sunning place for passing butterflies; dragonflies, too, patrolled this spot in August. Behind
the bank a stream of iron water, deep orange, seeped from
the ground and caused the grass to grow greener here than
anywhere else. In time the clough opened out and the fall of
water grew less boisterous, and channelled in gracious

curves, moved on to the river, yet there was no dalliance to its flow, and the hot sunshine dimpled and glanced on its surface. There were banks of pebbles here from which the imprisoning boulder clay had long since been washed away, and here showed a glimpse of the underlying out-crop of new red sandstone. Here where the humble bees zoomed in May grew the pink flowers of butterbur, for the land was better drained, and plants from the stream's higher reaches were no longer found. A small patch of gorse or a broom or two flowered fitfully through the four seasons and here grew the oak and there stood the beech in fully glory.

A hardwood dam athwart the stream lay channelling most of its waters into a large mill lodge, puddled well with clay and buttressed with old railway sleepers and lengths of old steel rails, the whole buried under a wide bank of enclosing earth and masonry. This was the plentiful soft water without which the bleaching and dyeing industry could never have taken place.

Up to the mid eighteenth century the bleaching of linen, later cotton, was a lengthy business. After steeping the cloth in an alkaline solution for several days (bucking) it was passed through rinsing water and exposed to the sun and elements in grassy meadows (crofting). This process was repeated several times, the whole action taking between six and eight months to complete. Whitefield where I attended Grammar School, is a place name that reveals its origins. Since we seem to have had light- fingered people always with us it will be understood that the safety of the cloth was under a continual hazard, and croft breaking was common though the penalty of being caught was death, one of the two-hundred-and-twenty-odd offences to which the death penalty was attached in this country in those days. The last man who suffered this fate seems to have been George Rus-sell who in 1798 was hanged on a gibbet in Newton Heath,

Stand Grammar School, Whitefield. Class V. A.H. 1938. We were told that Clive of India attended our school. The girls are as follows: Back row, from left: Annie Ralphson; Josie Ogden; Margery Buchanan; Helen Nuttall; —; Vivian Sampson; —. Front row: Edna Smith (my bosom pal "Muffin"); myself, Catherine Houghton; Miss Edith Hargreaves, form mistress and mathematics teacher; Jacqueline Colbert; Pauline Sampson; Eileen Freedman; Muriel Hadfield.

for breaking into Mr. Shorrock's croft. Towards the end of the century a new bleach of chlorine and lime began to be used, cutting down the time needed to complete the process, from months to days.

The bank had a road of river stones running alongside it and so well had this road been laid, keyed in some cunning way by a master hand, that it was quite impossible to pick out one single pebble without first shattering one. Years and years of wear, of human feet in clattering clogs and of the high-ringing rattle of the iron tyres of horse drawn drays had failed to make any rut or channel in the resistant surface. The sad, pitiful imitation of these modern times, stones set upright in concrete, seems more like a miniature tank trap set to tear off the slender heels of young ladies' shoes, the higher the more hazardous, and deadly for anyone on foot when the pebbles have a coating of black ice, is reminiscent, rather of blanched almonds stuck in marzipan by a tyro cook.

And so this broad road ran between the water and the mill buildings, bordered by gritstone kerbs set deep into the earth.

The buildings were old: three storeys high, brick built and having windows of many-paned glass, each floor above the ground being supported on cast iron pillars bearing square section wooden beams upon which the smaller, oblong joists rested. Years of steady maintenance in the days of plenty had preserved the fabric wonderfully well on the whole. Applications of pitch, coat upon coat, covered the mild steel railings surrounding the walls so that, beneath, they were as newly erected. A wooden bell tower fitted with louvres but from which the bell had long since been removed, stood above the roof, also pitch black, though its pyramidal apex where the droppings of so many birds showed white offered stark contrast. Limewash had been freely used in the interior. What artificial lighting had originally been used it was hard to conjecture, but a primitive system of electric cables borne upon white porcelain insulators ran the wall perimeter.

Two casualties of neglect, a pair of ancient keirs, vertical cylindrical tanks, solidly constructed of rivetted boiler plates, stood side by side, thick laminates of rust peeling from them.

The pointed railings which kept us away from the keirs lapped the buildings on three sides, but on the third section

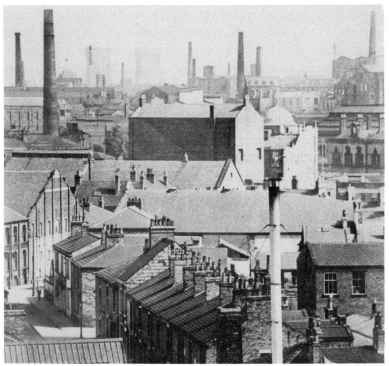

Tall mill chimneys epitomised Lancashire sixty years ago. From the hill in Heaton Park the highest chimney of all at Royton was visible. When Wakes Weeks came and the factories shut down you could see for miles in the clear air. There was a cotton mill in Newtown Street where I was born. The children used to creep up and gaze aghast at the immense furnace. I tagged along with my brothers and the inferno later haunted my dreams.

they entered the main wall by the bleaching shed, and with a chained gate which guarded the fixed bridge of railway sleepers, denying entrance to the stranger.

Down in the yard stood carboys of corrosive chemicals, the freshness or otherwise of the straw packing showing the time that had elapsed since they had been left there, and beside them, a dozen or so fifty gallon steel drums, supine and full or upright and empty.

During those hot, endless August afternoons in the Summer school holiday as daily we stripped the white convolvulus flowers off the railings, swallows rested momentarily above us then swept off, cleaving paths across the cool running water, and jackdaws crying, wheeled and tumbled in the air. As the hours passed swifts began to ascend, screaming and rising in vast circles until lost to sight.

As day followed day the rose bay willow herb lifted higher than the surrounding grasses. Its paleness slowly changed to pink, then to mid magenta. Earth dried in the golden hours of sunlight and in advancing heat zephyrs sprang up and raised tiny dust whirls. Small copper butterflies fluttered above the flowering thistles; common browns patrolled the verges.

At times a door stood open and there was a glimpse of shafting and driving belts, and a skip or two on a loading bay, holding grey cloth, but seldom did anyone came to bustle about the area. On other occasions a labourer in brat and cloth cap and with shirt sleeves rolled to his elbows passed through the yard on some errand or other, or bearing on his shoulder a bolt of cloth. We could see and hear work going on in the building but never did anyone come and ask us why we lingered or sent us about our business.

And so the years passed slowly, and change itself was correspondingly slow and scarcely to be noticed, but change there was. The loaded drays became less frequently employed and the loads themselves diminished so that the green tarpaulins sagged hollow-cheeked over the dray centre bar. The sounds of industry grew less and at times the shafting was not moving, but an open window showed that there was life still inside. Labour no longer came to clean the windows, those many sparkling panes, and cobwebs, picked out in cotton lint dust increased in thickness, and flies, moths and an odd unfortunate wasp hung there in gossamer chains, pulsating in the wind, and thicker and yet more thicker grew the webs inside. Birds with increasing temerity nested over the dyehouse clerestories: if a slate slid off the roof it was no longer replaced. The loading bay remained unswept and oats dropped from the nosebag of the solitary dray horse blown by winds into some favourable seeding place, took root, flourished and bore harvest in the cracks and fissures of the way.

Kearsley's was at least a mile away from the village, at the end of a long, winding country lane, passing a country house, or a few cottages and a large farm if one kept religiously to the path. One could see the mill buildings in the shallow valley about a couple of furlongs before reaching it and here the lane forked, continuing to the mill but taking the right fork if one wished to end up at a rival establishment, well, hardly rival since it was so much more bustling, modern, efficient and of course, larger. This rival was Dewhurst's, and Dewhurst's bore as much relationship to Kearsley's as a modern hypermarket bears to an old-fashioned grocer's with the owner-assistant behind the counter in a large white apron and a personal approach.

Dewhurst's catchment area for their water supply sprang from the base of an escarpment of almost pure sand overlaid with boulder clay, the bank or raised terrace of the original river course and now a quarter mile from the river and running parallel with it for several miles. This was another favourite playground, for the steam provided us with minnows, and we wandered along its meanders under the oaks and beeches, and through the dark, glossy green grasses — called sheep's fescue tussocks — the tips of each clump, a mass of hair-like grass blades, turned brown in Autumn, and they yielded long flowering 'Silver Spoons' valued by girls when out collecting wild flowers for home. Bordered yellow underwing months were common here, and occasionally a weak-winged cinnabar moth in early September. I have seen shrews amongst this grass though I had not yet found a nest other than a warbler's nest. Where the grass thinned the "sourdabs", our name for sorrel, spread, together with tormentil, in the impoverished soil. There was an approach for pedestrians only fenced by beech boughs, split lengthways with steel wedges and raised on square cut oak posts, and since there was no transport to either mill except one's own bicycle, very few of the staff owned cars, this path was the one generally favoured by workers.

On terminating my school life one Friday afternoon in July, the following day I was offered my first job at De-whurst's. I learned something about its history then. Founded about the time of the First World War, probably dyeing khaki cloth the place had steadily extended by using modern techniques and up-to-date machinery, and increasing the variety of cloth treatments, especially to supply the feminine demand for man-made fibres textiles. The place would have gone on from strength to strength but for one thing: the draught of the 1930s economic blizzard had already begun to strike rigid many of the older industries on which the prosperity of the nation depended. Some, of course, never woke from this icy sleep of death: cotton was feeling the cold strongly and India was turning out miles of her own textiles for home consumption. Every Monday morning one could see the effects of trade recession in the queue of unemployed labourers lined up outside the general office, hoping, and a slim hope it was, of being

Market Street, Bolton. A town of atmosphere, as I remember it. "Bradleys, the Great Clothiers", had shops all over Lancashire, catering for the working classes. Their stock-in-trade must have been men's cloth caps. Grandmother said some operatives never took them off their heads and this, in her opinion, caused baldness. Kenyon's on the left was another popular outfitter's. On the right Brown's Summer Sale is in full swing.

engaged. It could be seen in the works itself, in the silent bleaching sheds every Monday and Tuesday, for only on the next three days of the week did the place become alive; there wasn't enough work to last the whole week.

By seven every morning I signed on the office staff book by which time the labouring staff had been at their tasks an hour. At eight the stridency of the steam whistle brought a temporary stop to work and ushered in breakfast for the next thirty minutes, ten of which were wasted because of the poor facilities for providing drink; one had to queue up and there were but two lanes of workers. At that identical hour the Chairman of the company rang through to the office. I had to receive the call, for some person I knew not but who was somewhere in that complex of buildings. It could be a wild goose chase, and it often was. Punctually an hour later, coinciding with the arrival of the typists arrived also the Chairman. As this was my first essay into real work I found that I was feeling rather jaded by four-thirty in the afternoon when the typists drank their afternoon tea — there was none for the clerks — and if, after the hooter had sounded "down tools" and I still had to wait upon the Chairman at his private residence two miles away — get there under my own steam, and wait until he signed the mail, I would arrive home about the time I should have been beginning my first Commercial class at night school. That time was seven-thirty, and I had still to eat my evening meal, the first food since twelve-thirty. As I sat in **his** kitchen, empty as the proverbial drum, a cook would open the Esse oven and take out a large roasting tin in order to baste the capon it contained. I won't pursue the trend of thought I held then, I'm sure that you can easily guess. I should also point out, that I occupied that job for six months before I was allotted a chair. It was probably assumed, and quite truthfully in fact, that I would be too much occupied with important matters pertaining to my place of employment than to allow my mind to stray on to the fleshy temptation of sitting and giving my legs a rest. Unused to such treatment I soon developed the painful symptoms of foot stress, fallen arches. Beyond provoking ribaldry from some quarters I was given no sympathy, not even by my doctor who merely questioned my lack of stamina, and that was all. At work I gathered brickbats, never bouquets, but that seemed to be the lot of the office drudge in those wretched days.

Several times a day I moved round the buildings distributing or collecting cyclostyled sheets pertaining to each order and the processes demanded for the same. From bleach house to merceriser; grey room to singe house; stenter one to stenter two and on to direct dye, vat dye and fancy dye with their rows of triangular steel troughs and vast vat where man-made textile fabrics tumbled in steaming troughs of solutions and so on to white callender sheds one and two and on to finishing room and make-up rooms until I knew each cloth process from memory. To see an endless, wet, twisted rope of cloth hurtling at so many miles per hour through a series of porcelain eyes from room to room and fed into the insatiable maw of vertical or horizontal keir was exhilarating, and the smells there added to that infection: the pungent nip on the nostrils of singed cotton nap; the unpleasantness of chlorine in the bleach house mingling with the vinegary draughts from next door, the merceriser, and oh, the sweatiness in the stenter!

The directors were related to each other, all members of one family, father, sons, cousins, uncle and alas, I seemed to rattle the lot. Pity I pray, pity for gauche youth fallen amongst you! I jostled the elder son in passing him (he was twice as big as I was and furthermore had a Director's backside); I kept the younger son, Master Cedric, waiting, WAITING on the 'phone far too long when searching for him, for a man who was off work ill. I gave the answers to the Chairman's enquiries in a way he considered unsuitable. They were straight and direct, though never impertinent, but they were not tempered with the right amount of smooth approach, of studied deference as befitted one in my humble station. Worst of all I kept uncle waiting, for his tea, and that was unforgivable. Actually I was detained in the making-up room waiting for an urgent order to be made ready for the Chairman, but I should have got the tea before going. It was no use saying that on principle he refused his tea before the time dictated. Basically I had to be taught the "right attitude" to my Employer, and that was enough. The employer's decision was final, in those days. Uncle was put out; Uncle was cross; Uncle threatened to fire me there and then, but he slowly relented, or rather, it occurred to him he hadn't asked the Chairman's approval first. But . . . but, if it happened again . . .! It didn't happen again, for within the week Uncle had left us for other spheres. He suddenly died.

I had feared that I would get into his bad books again but there was no need to worry; my fate at this establishment had already been decided. Of course, I had to go, and before I was sixteen and thus liable for an Insurance stamp, and a minimal rise in salary, and I was dismissed without notice whilst the job passed to a fourteen year old boy whose father habitually supported the bar in the Chairman's club. The letter of dismissal arrived on Good Friday (yes, post **was** delivered on that day then) and I was so stunned I stayed away from church, or perhaps was taken on a picnic to help me forget. I was such an innocent that I believed I had failed to hold down a job, the inadmissible fault amongst the hard-working artisan class. It was so difficult to find a job at that time that to lose one's employment was tantamount to a dereliction of duty.

During this initial job I began to be aware of the pettiness of the adult mind and the animosity, even to the point of frightening malevolence that seemed to, as it were, exude from one or two older people. Adults, it appeared to me had a built-in dislike of many of their fellow humans, and their peevishness could be every bit as great as that of a child, and last far, far longer. A postman, by mistake, had brought to the works a small bottle of dye that was addressed to Kearsley's. The Secretary passed it to me and directed that it should be returned to the Post Office. Yet when I innocently suggested that it would be easier and more helpful if I took it across to the other place on my way home I was answered with a frown and, "You will do as you are told, and on no account will you deliver it to the other place", almost as though I had suggested something most reprehensible like compounding a felony.

And so I left for good my first place of employment on Maundy Thursday, and for forty years I never set foot near the place, then by chance finding myself on my native heath again — it was again Good Friday — I paced the old road.

Along the clough and towards the river I trod, and at first it seemed that little had changed; the old vistas were still recognisable. There was Kearsley's, looking a little older, and a few things were missing, but substantially the same. It was still in use though not for dyeing and bleaching. I turned towards the river, and there was Dewhurst's, and though all the buildings seemed to be there the place was dead; all was locked and barred, and had been for many a long year. "Oh, that place?" said a passer-by, "it's a warehouse or depository of sorts: it was a busy works in the old days, but that was long before my time."

I smiled and thought a little, and then turned my back to it.

CHAPTER 9

Music Hath Charms and Curtain Up

WE came from a music-loving family. Great Grand-father Houghton queued a great length of time and at high cost to hear Jenny Lind sing, though he had never learned to play a musical instrument beyond a rough and ready rendering with two fingers in the right hand and basic chords in the left. He had, and so had father, a bursting budget of songs of every description that we learned from memory by his singing. Some were very revealing of the type of song taught in the elementary schools established under the Compulsory Education of Forster's Act of 1870. "Murmur gentle lyre" moved to a song of cricket and a setting of Felicia Hemans: "Trembling now the lily weeps, faded the roses shiver." There were reminders of Charles Lamb, Blake and Kingsley and their concern for boy chimney sweeps:

> Sweep, sweep cries little Jack
> With brush and bag upon his back.
> . . . He once was pretty Jack
> And had a kind mama . . .
> But foolish child he ran away . . .

*Irwell Springs, Bacup, winners of the Thousand Guineas Trophy and Gold
Medals. Brass bands were very much a part of childhood as they turned up
at Prestwich Carnival and attended all the Whitsuntide Walks. We would
also be awakened by them on Christmas Eve as we snuggled warm in bed.
The glorious strains of carols sung by the massed choirs of Waits floated up
the street. One Christmas I fell asleep after the Waits and the band had
departed and woke to find half of my chocolate Noah's Ark animals consumed by hungry brothers. One of my mother's relations played in this
Bacup band.*

"What was Mama doing to allow such a state of affairs?" I
reasoned, whilst flaxen-haired baby Sheila, who understood the song perfectly well, cried her eyes out. However,
that did not stop father from doing it again. Many of
father's songs were harrowing but "My Grandfather's
Clock", I have learned since, was even popular in the
United States. It was taught to the children of Bethesda
Street, Burnley, a century ago and the headmaster recorded
in his log book that the children sang it with enthusiasm.

This spate of music could not fail to have effect. Charlie
joined the Anglican choir and learned to play the piano.
Vaughan Williams was Music Editor of the English Hym-
nal, the book which he used, and with this and the Cathe-
dral Psalter he learned to point the psalms, getting a good

My sister Sheila, beloved, insep-arable companion. We shared everything including tummy ache on Walking Days which were often freezing cold. A spinster to this day, Sheila became an artist and College Lecturer.

basic training which led eventually to post of Head of Music and church organist.

Charlie's piano was not a new one although a later model than those with fretwork fronts, scarlet ruched silk backings and candelabra. Called a cottage piano and having a wooden frame, its tone was delicate and hesitant on some keys as one might expect from a genteel old lady in figured walnut who had known better times. It suffered also from piano arthritis. Several of its jacks would, at moments of stress, totter from their upper parts and cause the hammers to fall back on their strings. To prevent this movement strips of pink sticking plaster were affixed to the damaged members, rendering touch a little uneven, but sound was still there. I distinctly remember a man with horse and cart taking it away, my parents having sold it for three pounds when, for Charlie's benefit, we graduated to a German overstrung which weighed a ton. There was also a revolving piano stool which stood in for merry-go-round when inspiration flagged. We children whirled round upon it in turns in an ecstasy of revolutions which brought on dizzy "dos".

The toy that Charlie had loved most was a cheap tin musical box emitting four faint notes, a theme of many possibilities, germ of melodies yet unheard. Perhaps it set him off in his exploration of music. As he sat quietly turning the handle and listening did he hear "the horns of

Elfland faintly blowing?" Certainly it was on Christmas Eve
that through the crisp night air we both heard a ravishing
sound. The Congregational Chapel Choir annually bor-
rowed a wooden motor pantechnicon and using its natural
resonance for their singing and for shelter when the
weather was bad, toured the parish, rendering Christmas
carols. This competent choir awakened us to the seasonal
hymn "Christians awake, salute the happy morn." The
amazing sweetness and wonder of this moment was akin,
years later, to the seconds after my daughter was born in a
Catholic nursing home. As I was wheeled towards the
ward, "Hail Marys" cadenced echoingly.

What I know of the real McCoy theatre, until recently, I
thought, came from my stage-struck father and grandfather. By the time this interest rubbed off on me, black and
white silent films, soon to be followed by "the talkies", had
arrived, causing some young women to feel emancipated if
they smoked 'Casket' cigarettes, "delightful to inhale, threepence a packet". For me, emancipation meant visiting the
"flea pit". I'm quite sure about the fleas for I found one
snugged down in the sleeve of my jumper after "Les En-
fants du Paradis". Theatre management did its best, sluicing
down pink marble corridors resembling brawn, with Jeyes
Fluid seven days a week, the fumes from which fought des-
perately with the reek of tobacco smoke, but this did not
deter; nor did the long ride by bus on what always seemed
a wet, greasy afternoon.

Once in my worn, red plush, tip-up seat, raptly following
the black and white flicker of wicked Ambrose persecuting
mediaeval witches, or Arletty and Jean-Louis Barrault
adorning sets reminiscent of Impressionist paintings, I was
lost to the world. Father had been hopelessly stage and
cinema struck, but mother's side were Wesleyan Methodists,
denied drinking, dancing and theatre, so it was against
fearful odds, which in early years involved diligent if fur-

The year of "On the Rocks" when war was declared and Edward joined up. This photograph of myself at seventeen was taken by father's friend Carl Cloud who had a Studio in Oxford Street, Manchester. A generous man, Carl Cloud brightened dad's life at Christmas and ten years later took my wedding photographs.

tive recovery of pop bottle deposits that I scraped together ninepence of two and sixpence to see Robert Donat in "The Doctor's Dilemma" and Olivier and Richardson in "The Government Inspector". Fifty years on, that seemed a bargain, especially with names like Fonteyn, Helpman and Gielgud and such plays as Ghosts, Precious Bane, Candida, Mrs. Warren's Profession, Lady Windermere's Fan; such companies as D'Oyley Carte, Covent Garden, Royal Carl Rosa and the Old Vic.

Thoughts slide to fifty years ago. Treading the dusty boards of an attic, surrounded by shabby Victorian bric-a-brac and the detritus of a century brought back memories like a throng of unruly children screaming for attention. I had thought the attics of Britain swept clean by demands for charity shops, car boot and jumble sales, but here lay one subject to no wind of change. Here had lived a distant relative close to my heart, a fact made obvious by cogent evidence.

Passing over feathered boas, antimacassars and lurching bamboo plant stands, I delved into the paper work. There were old Christmas cards of great charm, visiting and birth-day cards expressing the gentle humour of a pre-war era, but most interesting of all were the masses of theatre pro-grammes from which leapt great names and record perfor-mances: Enrico Caruso; Madame Patti; Martin Harvey; Clara Butt; Harcourt Beattie; Ronald Bayne; Mrs. General Tom Thumb and the American Lilliputian Company — even Pantomime, complete with "every child's dream", the Transformation Scene. My ears filled with the thunder of clapping hands, as in mind's eye, lit by limelight, rich-red velvet curtains braided with heavy gold, rose and fell like yo-yos.

Small advertisements alongside the evening's entertain-ment added further interest, not to mention commanding documentation: "Consult Madame Blanche, corset special-ist, for unbreakable Empirella steels;" "Wear Dunn's famous hats"; "Do not be without Veldtic Boots", but a glowering hint of things to come cropped up in the most sensational play of the year on Monday March 21st, 1921, "The Right to Strike".

Out of this cornucopia there fell a solitary dance pro-gramme, deckle-edged, with its slim, white pencil dangling. The date was arresting: November 24, my birthday, but the year was 1899. Twenty dances with French-sounding titles were printed in two neat columns, but the pristine paste-board was devoid of partners' names. Perhaps it was years later that my ancestor wrote on the back: "I did not learn to dance." The same hand informed her parents when she left Lytham for Goodson's drapers in Deansgate, Manchester: "I knew everything at the shop on the first day so I am not too tired but we do not close until 9 o'clock at night." With infectious enthusiasm she also wrote to a soldier friend, Arthur, about Mrs. Patrick Campbell: "Have you seen her? she was born in 1855 and was the first Eliza Dolittle."

Ethel, I mused, must have been my father's age, but

whereas he loved the friendly, boisterous atmosphere of the Alexandra Music Hall, later the "Tiv." or Tivoli Theatre, and such spectacular occasions as The Wild West Coming to Town, she gloried in plays and opera. To the Royalty Theatre and Opera House came Gilbert and Sullivan when the D'Oyley Carte in their tour northwards stopped off in 1899. In constrast, when Buffalo Bill's Circus came to the Hippodrome on September 21st, 1904, Colonel Cody brought 500 horses, choking the area with people, wagonettes, landaus and horse-drawn trams.

To the intrepid Ethel, devotee of "Curtain Up", distance was no object. In her ankle-length, blue, Devon serge skirt she sped by train or horse bus, after a working week of sixty hours, to see Henry Irving in "The Bells" or the fabled Miss Fortescue in "Moths". No time for dancing! Ever-changing theatre was her glamorous escape route. The programme bore witness, notes in the margins widening her admiration and enjoyment.

Dust motes swarmed in a sudden gleam of sunshine brightening the grimy fanlight. It was high time to leave the attic which I had entered as a stranger but where I had found a friend. Across the gulf of a century I saluted this stage-struck lass, distant blood-sister of mine. "Oranges, cakes, sweets, programmes, a penny each!" "The play's the thing!" Was that an echo down the years? No doubt about it; the lure of the footlights was in the family genes.

CHAPTER 10

On the Rocks

I WAS never a dedicated rock climber, rather more of a "hanger on", if you will excuse the pun. Although not, in my young days, a sufferer from vertigo, the discomfort of aching limbs driven over and over again to new effort when early energy had already been expended, did not appeal to this hedonist. Dewdrops dripping from the nose end, wet clothing clinging to shrinking limbs, these things militated against the sport, although I did experience the joy of wet-scented greenery bruised by crampons, grass, fern, heather and the like all around, of moss caught under questing finger nails along pitifully narrow ledges, of the sheer grittiness of millstone grit under the palms, moist wind on the face and on the up and up, the sound of water falling far below. After several attempts at a girdle traverse, I clung to the spirit of the sport rather than to the letter. Whilst my brother and his companions sweated alternately with heat and fright I found myself a convenient sheltered ledge and painted the scene. On this same ledge on one occasion we all crouched during a thunder storm, watching with fascination the blue lightning sparking and bouncing from the metal hairpins of one of our party. Thus, rock climbing for me became essentially a spring and summer pastime, but vividly I remember my last attempt before discovering, most sensibly, my true metier.

We had decided to spend a New Year's Day on a line of low "cliffs" and though it was cold, the slate and stones were dry so we set off from Stonethwaite. However, within the hour soft, persistently fine drizzle began, the type of rain that when set in, seems to go on for days. Nevertheless we continued, passing not a soul in the swirling mist. Our clattering boots stormed over rocky outcrops, drenched through dubs, doused in oozy peat hags, squelched sedge and sucked tussocks. Through springing heaths and slippery skirtings of snagging furze and whins, at long last we reached our goal. We were wet, yes we were wet, but we set about what we had come to do in the way that only young people can. Came the meal break, "Where's the sandwiches?" asked my brother Edward, whose heroes were Eric Shipton and Edward Whymper.

"You should have them," I said heavily. The air, besides being misty, became suddenly blue as brotherly insult was

Catherine, Charles and Sheila (foreground) have scaled a huge erratic boulder on Penmon beach. The four of us walked miles every day, whilst mother slaved away over the primitive cottage stove to produce delicious meals. Edward taught us a lot about birds. We four revelled in being in the wilds but father grumbled and sang "Oh for the wings of a dove" to fly back to the mucky city. The year was 1934.

hurled in my direction. Our two companions nobly shared their butties, but we were left half empty rather than half full.

The last climb of the day found me deeply dispirited and I withdrew shiveringly. The final pitch took far longer than expected as all three were tired and hungry and we left the rock face amidst silence and approaching darkness. The paths were now muddy rivulets and the sedges shuddering quagmires of despair. Looking back on it, I think we must have all been mad. In the darkness far ahead a tiny pinpoint of light moved steadily towards us and eventually a man clad in oilskins, carrying a hand lamp arrived. "What on earth are you doing out on a night like this?" he said, shaking raindrops around like a shaggy dog. He was a water bailiff and had to be out whatever the weather.

Two years earlier my sister and I had a similar experience trudging Honister Pass in a snowstorm. The men at the slate quarry asked us the same question. It was around Christmas time and we were allowed to shelter and rest up a while in a

Napes Needle, Lake District. In our teens we explored the Lake District widely, climbing Great Gable; Esk Hawes; Green Gable; Red Pike; Haystacks; Coniston Old Man. Edward and friends Alan Clixby, George Coates and Brian Dilworth, having climbed the Wetterhorn, were at a mountain hut in Switzerland when war was declared in 1939. They descended to find every visitor gone. The British Consul took them overland by car to Paris en route for home.

hut, where I suspect they kept the dynamite. Those workmen were equally astonished and must also have thought us mad, but I shall never forget, on that occasion, before the storm had blown up and the dusk approached, those wondrous blue shadows in the gullies of Haystacks and on the snow fields of Robinson.

At last, very tired and gently stewing in our own juices, since the rain had stopped and a warm, wet wind had sprung up, we reached Rosthwaite. All doors were closed; a few lights behind curtains or blinds were showing, but the village had a deserted, call-tomorrow look.

Suddenly, all four of us stopped in our tracks, noses lifted to the wind, all in the same direction, like the famous Bisto Kids of that now long ago advertisement. A delectable smell wafted towards us, causing our empty stomachs to rumble and lurch drunkenly as the gastric juices overflowed. It was the smell of freshly-baked bread. Like the famous kids (Ah! Bisto), we allowed the odour to permeate our nostrils. Breathing in deeply, we followed the trail round a corner and into a tiny court where stood an open door ablaze with rosy light from within. The heart-warming odours drifted from a great, black, glowing fire oven.

"I haven't got much," said the cheerful soul in charge. "The bread is still in the oven, but I have some steak pies left over from lunch. I've a few pasties too and there's plenty of hot tea. Don't sit there in wet clothes. Take your coats and jackets off. It's warm in here with the oven on. Get a wash at the sink. There's soap and a roller towel . . . it will do for all of you."

Absorbing warmth, relaxing weary muscles, basking in glow, we perched on wooden stools, taking in the satisfying ambience of a Lake District kitchen, steadily munching and drinking tea in huge, white mugs decorated with blue bands. The world was a wonderful place and we would not have missed our outing for the world — now it was over! "I like to see good appetites," said our Borrowdale benefactress. "Wouldn't go on t 'tops myself, but

Coniston was in Lancashire when we had a week's holiday in this L.M.S. Camping Coach in 1937. What a revelation to see clean sparrows and clear running water in the becks! Each morning the friendly station staff brought a locomotive up the line carrying cans of water, our daily supply. It chuffed alongside in a fury of steam, stopping by the carriage door. Another revelation!

some do well off it. Are you sure you wouldn't like another fill-up?" Indeed our thirsts were unslakeable.

It must have been the steak pies and the fruit pasties of this guardian angel that settled me thereafter for the good Life rather than the quivering quagmires of the high fells. To the four winds of heaven went the rope, the crampons and tri-counis in exchange for the perfume, the flowers and the candy. To this day, however, I never pass through Rosthwaite without thinking of Mrs. Towers, her second-nature kindness, common sense, cooking prowess, rich Cumbrian accent and sparkling Mr. Pickwick spectacles. There is involved even essential Wordsworth:

"*She was a phantom of delight*
When first she gleamed upon my sight."

Within a few months of that outing, the last we had together, Hitler marched into Poland, without a by your leave and our world was never the same again. It was the end of childhood.

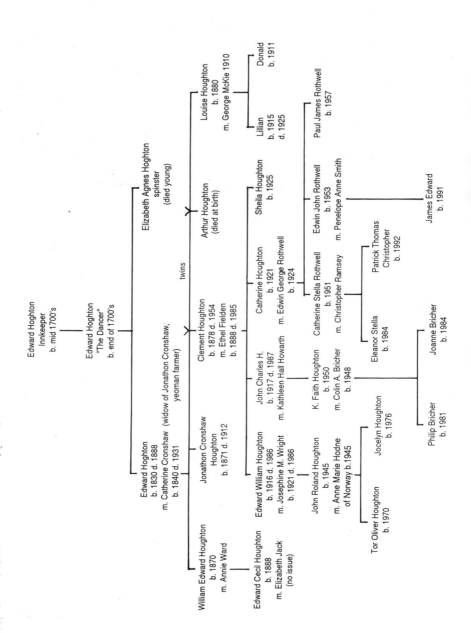